A PHOT

ECUADOR
AND
GALAPAGOS

CLIVE BYERS

NEW HOLLAND

First published in 2009 by
New Holland Publishers (UK) Ltd
London • Cape Town • Sydney • Auckland

www.newhollandpublishers.com

Garfield House, 86–88 Edgware Road, London W2 2EA, United Kingdom

80 McKenzie Street, Cape Town 8001, South Africa

Unit 1, 66 Gibbes Street, Chatswood, New South Wales, Australia 2067

218 Lake Road, Northcote, Auckland, New Zealand

10 9 8 7 6 5 4 3 2 1

ISBN 978 1 84773 140 1

Senior Editor: Krystyna Mayer
Design: Bob Johnson
Cartography: Stephen Dew
Production: Melanie Dowland
Commissioning Editor: Simon Papps
Editorial Direction: Rosemary Wilkinson

Reproduction by Modern Age Repro House Limited, Hong Kong
Printed and bound in Malaysia by Times Offset (M) Sdn Bhd

CONTENTS

INTRODUCTION

Although Ecuador is one of the smallest countries in South America and has a microscopic land area by South American standards, it has enormous biodiversity, which includes one of the largest bird lists in the world.

THE REGION'S GEOGRAPHY

The huge biodiversity of this small country essentially hinges on a unique combination of two critical factors: firstly, the equator running east to west just north of the capital, Quito, and secondly the fact that the Andean mountain range runs the length of the country, splitting it north to south. These factors lend mainland Ecuador four important zoogeographical zones:

1. The littoral zone of the coast (La Costa).

2. The western lowlands extending from the Andean foothills to the coast.

3. The Andean mountain range.

4. The mostly forested eastern Amazonian lowlands.

A fifth 'life zone' is the oceanic territory in which the Galapagos Islands lie, roughly 1,000km to the west of the mainland. Because it is so isolated and uniquely different from continental Ecuador, the Galapagos archipelago is dealt with separately on page 10.

THE ENVIRONMENT & CONSERVATION

It is widely regarded that the presence of a strong bird population is an important indicator of a healthy environment. However, as is increasingly and very worryingly the case, the opposite is true. In lowland Ecuador deforestation is rampant and ongoing, devastating the environment but apparently unstoppable. This is for a variety of reasons, just one of which is widespread poverty. In an overwhelmingly Catholic country, the problem of runaway population growth is another very serious threat to the environment. Deforestation continues apace as young people seek land to farm and a living for their often very large families.

There are other reasons for the catastrophic destruction of Ecuador's fabulous natural resources. The vested interests of the wealthy few are rapidly destroying those resources, but the major offenders are the logging companies that are making a fast buck, regardless of the consequences. It is down to the biggest players with the power to stop the outrageous plundering of the forests of this remarkable little country.

Poorly controlled operations by oil companies have also wreaked considerable harm on this once pristine environment. As a result, many parts of Oriente province in the eastern lowlands are badly polluted at ground level. As the oil giants raced to exploit their goals they did not worry about cleaning up their mess; for many indigenous people it was too late to protect their lands, as corporate powers ran roughshod over the local population.

However, it is not all bleak, and there is hope. Many people, foreigners and Ecuadorian nationals alike, have taken up the cudgel to defend the environment and protect the interests of the local population. Some have bought blocks of the forested eastern lowlands that are so sought after by multinational oil corporations.

Native people have fought back by stealth and cunning to reclaim their territories and thus protect their vulnerable forests, which are home to a multitude of bird species and myriad other animals and plants. For instance, the Waorani people inhabiting the eastern lowlands of Ecuador have successfully fought to protect some of their ancestral property from these corporate raiders.

Cultural and environmental tourism is thriving in Ecuador and many people make a living by welcoming birders to savour the avian delights of this wonderful country. Some Ecuadorians have become bird guides because of the growth in this 'ornithological industry'. Many of them are highly skilled, particularly in their amazing knowledge of bird calls and song. They can now share their knowledge, making a career out of showing tourists to Ecuador their fabulous birdlife rather than killing it.

WHERE TO WATCH BIRDS IN ECUADOR

There are so many localities to watch birds in this incredibly rich little country that it is difficult to know where to start. I have begun near the capital, Quito, and worked out from there. These days the Web has more information than you can imagine, and all of the companies, people and sites mentioned can be 'Googled' to obtain more information on the best bird-watching locations.

Yanacocha
Once acclimatized to the altitude, you may want to hire a taxi to take you up to this site on the Volcan Pichincha, which towers above the city. From downtown Quito it is a drive of about 45 minutes to reach the site, which is now protected and managed by the Jocotoco Foundation. An easy-level trail meanders through lovely cloud forest where you can see many montane species including (perhaps) the rare Black-breasted Puffleg, *Eriocnemis nigrivestis*. Rediscovered here after many years, this beautiful hummingbird has been adopted as the emblem of Quito city.

Pasochoa Reserve
This forest reserve is a gem. Close to Quito, it can be easily explored on a day trip, or you can stay over for the night in the little hostel there (by prearrangement). The reserve contains a large number of birds and easy trails, and is surrounded by lovely pastoral countryside that is strangely reminiscent of England in its general ambience, with dairy cows in the fields and wandering the narrow lanes. After admiring the cows you might have the privilege, if you are lucky, of admiring a Flammulated Treehunter, *Thripadectes flammulatus*, on one of the reserve's well-kept trails (you will probably see much more, even if you are not that lucky!).

Cotopaxi National Park
This one is unmissable, for a great many reasons. It has great birds, of course. This massive snow-capped, cone shaped mountain is also one of the highest active volcanos in the world and is the home of the splendid Ecuadorian Hillstar, *Oreotrochilus chimborazo*, and the elusive Rufous-bellied Seedsnipe, *Attagis gayi*. The Noble Snipe, *Gallinago nobilis*, occurs

around the lake shore. You will need your own transport to explore this site.

Papallacta Pass

It is an easy drive to this site, the high pass over the eastern ridge of the Cordillera on the road to Baeza and Tena. There is the chance of seeing condors and numerous other species of bird. On a clear day (mornings are best, of course), you can enjoy the spectacle that is the enormous snow-clad volcano Antisana. You can then continue along the road to beautiful accomodation either at the Papallacta Hot Springs or further on at Guango Lodge. Enjoy the hummingbirds at either of these sites or in the gardens at Papallacta Village, where Sword-billed Hummingbirds, *Ensifera ensifera*, visit the trumpet datura flowers.

The Loreto Road

This left-side turning off the main road from Quito to Baeza and Tena is famous for the possibility of seeing many scarce foothill birds that are hard to find elsewhere. It has an advantage of being close to a variety of accomodations. Continue another 20 or so kilometres to the left-side turning to Volcan Sumaco and explore further for upper-tropical goodies such as fruit-eaters and more.

Cabanas San Isidro

Situated close to the main Quito-Tena Road, this is a well-known site owned by renowned birder Mitch Lysinger, who knows as much about the birds of the region as anyone. Here is lower temperate, mid-altitude cloud forest with trails. The Cordillera de Haucamayos is nearby and is a good site for the lovely Black-billed Mountain-Toucan, *Andigena nigrirostris*. The trail is on the right heading towards Tena, below the summit and radio tower.

Tandayapa Valley

This is situated on the western slope of the Cordillera only an hour or so out of Quito. A road meanders up the valley, where there are several options for accomodation. One is the Tandayapa Bird Lodge at the bottom run by Tropical Birding (a special place for hummingbirds and antpittas). Another is Bellavista Lodge at the top of the valley at the junction with the old road to Mindo. Look out for the Toucan Barbet, *Semnornis ramphastinus*, and the Tanager Finch, *Oreothraupis arremonops*, among other rarities.

The Mindo Area

Great birding opportunities abound here. The old road to Mindo (also known as the Nono-Mindo Road), including the stretch around the Tandayapa junction, is very good. Wander down this road and you will perhaps see birds such as the bizarre and secretive Ocellated Tapaculo, *Acropternis orthonyx*, tufted-cheeks and treehunters. Also in the area are a number of properties where artificial feeding opportunities are presented to antpittas (which are notoriously difficult to see, of course).

Contact Neblina Tours to be put in touch with Angel Paz at Refugio Paz de las Aves, or alternatively email his English-speaking friend Hector at hectorclavijo@yahoo.com, telephone 099931507. The services of Vinicio Perez and Jane Lyons at 'Birdwatcher's House' are also highly recommended. Google Birdwatcher's House for information. Septimo Paraiso Lodge is also highly commended. Email info@septimoparaiso.co.

The Rio Napo

This major tributary of the Amazon is accessed by flights from Quito to the Napo port town of Puerto Francisco de Orellana (which is usually known by the rather more user-friendly name of 'Coca'). This is your starting point for visiting the lodges along the river, four of which – the Napo Wildlife Centre, Sani Lodge, Sacha Lodge and La Selva Lodge – are described below. Google Napo Lodges for information about others.

Napo Wildlife Centre

This is a great lodge in this wonderful area, with all the facilities required for birders and all-round naturalists. It includes a canopy tower and excellent trail system, as well as superb guides, and is run by the local indigenous people. Contact Neblina Forest, info@ neblinaforest.com, or during office hours telephone toll free from the United States, 1800 538 2149, freephone from the United Kingdom, 0808 23 41434.

Sani Lodge

This is another highly recommended lodge in the Rio Napo area, with great trails and a canopy tower to view treetop species such as cotingas. For more information contact Neblina Forest, or email info@sanilodge.com.

Sacha Lodge

This is a long-established lodge on the famous Napo River. It is much commended, with great trails and a tower giving good access to the canopy. Contact www.sachalodge.com.

La Selva Lodge

Yet another long-established lodge on the Napo River. Contact www.laselvajunglelodge.com.

Kapawi Lodge

This lovely lodge is located on a lagoon along the Pastaza River near the Peruvian frontier, and is close to areas of swamp and white-sand habitats. This lends it a number of scarce species not found in the Napo drainage, like the Pearly Antshrike, *Megastictus margaritatus*, and Ancient Antwren, *Herpsilochmus gentryi*. The rare Buckley's Forest-Falcon, *Micrastur buckleyi*, occurs around the lodge itself.

The lodge is run by the local Achuar tribe. It is rather remote, and it is accessed by light plane to the local grass airstrip (scary but fun). For further information, contact the website canodros@canodros.com.

Playa de Oro Lodge

This is situated in the north-western lowlands, and is also known as the Choco. A number of the endemic birds of the region, most found more commonly further north in Colombia, can be seen in the area. Contact tracy@touch thejungle.org. The lowland rainforest of Ecuador is in extreme peril. These people need our help!

Machalilla National Park

This reserve lies just inland off the coast of Manabi province and also encompasses the Isla de la Plata not far offshore. Boats can be hired to take you to the island, famous for its nesting seabirds. It is also the only place other than Isla Española on the Galapagos Islands where the rare Waved Albatross, *Phoebastria irrorata*, nests.

Buenaventura

This foothill forest habitat on the western slopes of the far south of Ecuador is home to the rare El Oro Parakeet, *Pyrrhu-*

ra orcesi. The Jocotoco Foundation maintains a small accomodation centre here.

Guayaquil Area
Only a few kilometres from the sprawling city of Guayaquil is the forest reserve of Cerro Blanco, which has a number of Tumbesian endemics and a few Great Green Macaws, *Ara ambiguus.* The Manglares-Churute Reserve is about 40 km to the south and is famous for its shorebirds, waders, Horned Screamers, *Anhima cornuta,* and Tumbesian endemics on the Churute Hills. The arid Santa Elena Peninsula to the west is renowned for its Peruvian Thick-knees, *Burhinus superciliaris,* and the lagoons and saltpans that attract numerous migrant shorebirds.

The Gualaceo-Limon Road
This road traverses the eastern Andean slope and drops through many levels of beautiful cloud forest. An excellent birding road, it is accessed from the city of Cuenca.

Las Cajas National Recreational Area
Just north of the city of Cuenca and very easily accessed, this is an 'easy' birding site and excellent for condors. In the beautiful mountain scenery, look for the local Tit-like Dacnis, *Xenodacnis parina,* in the Polylepis groves. You may even be fortunate enough to see the rare Violet-throated Metaltail, *Metallura baroni,* at higher levels.

Podocarpus National Park
This huge forested reserve is best accessed from Loja city (to visit the headquarters and trail systems at Cajanuma), or from the town of Zamora (to visit the lower levels such as Rio Bombuscara). It is a very exciting area but needs time to be fully appreciated. Contact Fundacion Arco Iris in Loja for more information, info@arcoiris.org.ec.

Tapichalaca/Quebrada Honda
Situated in the south of Ecuador, this is the home of the rare and only recently described Jocotoco Antpitta, *Grallaria ridgelyi.* The Tapichalaca Reserve is owned by the Jocotoco Foundation in order to protect this spectacular but elusive bird. For information, contact www.fjocotoco.org.

Cordillera del Condor
Little explored until recent times because of an ongoing territorial dispute with Peru, this area is now opening up as a major addition to the amazing list of great birding localities in Ecuador. This is principally due to the discovery of the rare and local Orange-throated Tanager, *Wetmorethraupis sterrhopteron,* in the upper Nangaritza Valley. The site can be visited with the guidance of the owners of the Cabanas Yankuam. Contact info@lindoecuadortours.com, or visit their website at www.lindoecuadortours.com.

Gorupe
A new lodge is being set up (2008) by the Jocotoco Foundation in the far south near Macara. This is intended to allow visitors to enjoy the birds of the Tumbesian dry forest.

PLANNING A TRIP

Check the general weather conditions for any particular month before you decide when to visit. The weather is variable and only partially predictable, but there are significant trends.

An 'El Niño' event could mean that over a period of several months any birding trip could – quite literally – be a washout. Consult an Ecuadorian tour operator, who should have the best advice on timing your visit.

Local knowledge is essential if you are a serious birder who wants to see the most species. Do your homework first. If you have never travelled to South America before, you will be like a fish out of water – and your birding mind will truly be blown because of the sheer number and variety of birds present. Use this little book to at least familiarize yourself with the various bird families you are likely to encounter.

In Ecuador it is entirely possible to plan your own itinerary and hire a car, with the freedom to change plans depending on conditions. However, if you are seriously interested in seeing as many species as possible, it is perhaps better to join an organized group, which means that you can share a guide. There are many very good native Ecuadorian bird guides now. One tour company run by indigenous people, Neblina Forest, has been operating for many years. See under Napo Wildlife Centre, page 7, for contact details and check the Internet for further information.

Most tour operators have all the groundwork done for you. They should have contingency plans in the event of adverse weather, or other matters out of their control and affecting plans. In Ecuador this could be anything from days of torrential rain, with landslides blocking your route, to earthquakes or volcanic eruptions. Exciting stuff, but rather inconvenient if you have a tight schedule.

You will need good binoculars. In Ecuador (as in anywhere in the tropics) they must be waterproof. A telescope and a tripod – again waterproof – are an option, but they will be a heavy addition to your luggage. They may also be of limited use in most forest situations, where encounters with birds are frequently fleeting.

Sound recordings of Ecuadorian birds should be acquired and learned, and if necessary used to carefully (see caution below) lure birds into your field of view, particularly in forest environments. There is considerable skill required in using these techniques. All the equipment can be sourced from 'WILDSOUNDS', which can also provide you with information about the latest product innovations, and may be able to provide advice on techniques to enable you to get the best results in the field. Contact www.wildsounds.com.

If you have a good guide with the necessary library of bird sounds you will not need to take recordings of the huge number of species you may encounter. There are many birds that you will be unlikely to see without using playback. The local guides know how to use this essential aid and also know when to stop. This is because it can present a risk to the birds, as its success is based on a perceived threat and without care can cause serious distress, sometimes to the point where birds desert their territory (this is especially the case with nocturnal species).

If you are using playback be aware of the dangers you pose to birds and exercise moderation at all times. Try and prepare yourself for a possible response so you can see the bird and then leave it alone.

Local guides will know what a particular bird is likely to do. They will be able to say that it may not stay for long, gauge its response to you, or that it will come in low, perhaps at eye level, or at mid-level or high up in the canopy. The best advice I can offer is to pay attention and follow instructions from your guide, and to be quick and ready. Bear in mind that your guide may not want to persist and continue harassing a bird unnecessarily – and rightly so.

THE GALAPAGOS ISLANDS

This extraordinary group of islands is best known for being the inspiration for Charles Darwin's work on his famous thesis, *The Origin of Species,* which was based on the remarkable evolutionary diversity of the aptly named Darwin's finches. This was, of course, and continues to be, the basis of our understanding of evolution. Although some still question Darwin's views, it is clear with scientific reasoning that he was, in fact, entirely correct.

The volcanic Galapagos Islands straddle the equator approximately 960km west off the mainland of Ecuador. The equator itself runs through the northern peninsula of the largest island, Isabela. The avifauna of the islands is very different from that of mainland Ecuador. No fewer than 28 endemic species and another 16 endemic subspecies occur here. Currently (2008) 152 bird species have been recorded, although the majority are migrants or vagrants, with only 60 or so being resident.

The islands, although far remote from mainland Ecuador, are politically part of that country, and anyone wishing to visit has to transit through the capital, Quito, unless arriving by ship, boat or private yacht.

Most people are probably familiar with seeing images of the birds of the littoral zone (shore). This is, of course, a very important habitat on the Galapagos Islands for a number of species including the Lava Heron, *Butorides sindevalli,* and the world's rarest gull, the Lava Gull, *Larus fuliginosa.*

Inland from the shore the habitats of the lower elevations tend to be generally dry, becoming more humid and thus more heavily vegetated as you climb to higher altitudes. This is a reflection of the amount of rainfall or fog that these higher slopes receive. The lower levels are generally dominated by arid-tolerant plants and shrubs such as cacti and acacias. Palo Santo, *Bursera graveolens,* trees are the emergent feature here. The majority of the endemic land birds are found in these lower, drier areas. Numerous land birds are also found in the higher, often grassy, 'transition zone', where rainfall is higher and cattle are grazed.

At even higher elevations, certain specific habitat types include the 'Scalesia zone'. This habitat is essentially forest, dominated by the endemic *Scalesia pedunculata* trees, and is important for a number of bird species. These trees can grow to a height of up to 20m – somewhat unusual for islands, which are generally thought to be relatively arid and barren.

On Santa Cruz and San Cristobal the higher, wetter altitudes are dominated by the *Miconia robinsoniana* shrub. This habitat provides succour to fewer species than the forested lower slopes. More impoverished still is the highest and wettest habitat known as the Pampa zone, which consists essentially of grassland with emergent Galapagos Tree Ferns, *Cyathea weatherbyana,* up to 3m tall. Although it supports few species it is an important habitat for the endemic Galapagos Rail, *Laterallus spilonotus.*

Last, but certainly not least, are the seabirds. The archipelago is the recipient of the northernmost remnants of the cold Humboldt current. This brings food-rich water to the islands, which support large numbers of seabirds, including the world's only flightless cormorant, the only albatross that breeds on the equator and even a penguin that fishes in the northern hemisphere. The Galapagos Islands are truly a remarkable place.

11

Species Descriptions

Galapagos Penguin *Spheniscus mendiculus* 48-52cm

birdholidays.co.uk

This is a member of the group known as the burrowing penguins. However, this particular species finds little opportunity to burrow, as it lives on rocky lava shores and instead utilizes rock crevices in which to nest. It is extraordinary in several ways – it is the only penguin that nests on the equator and the only one that forages at sea in the northern hemisphere. It has been recorded as far north as the waters off Panama. Like the other Galapagos seabirds, it utilizes the northern extremity of the Humboldt current with its cold, food-rich water to survive here. Its total population is only a few thousand birds, and in some years only a few hundred pairs breed. It is susceptible to the trauma of El Niño events and is officially classed as Vulnerable.

Great Tinamou *Tinamus major* 43cm

A large, ground-dwelling bird, the Great Tinamou is common in various types of lowland forest east of the Andes and locally in north-western Ecuador. The beautiful far-carrying calls that accelerate to high-pitched trills are the evidence of this secretive bird's presence, and it is more often heard than seen. A relatively large body and long, thin neck and head are typical of the bigger members of the tinamou family. The large eyes are an indication of a tinamou's crepuscular life in the dark forests of the Amazon basin. It can be seen along the trails close to some of Ecuador's forest lodges, and occurs in both terra firma and Várzea habitats.

Pied-billed Grebe *Podilymbus podiceps* 28–30cm

Jim Walford

This small, stocky grebe is one of the most ubiquitous members of the family in both North and South America. It is instantly recognizable in the breeding season by its thick, whitish bill with the distinctive black band across it, which gives the bird its name. At this time it looks rather handsome, with its dark head contrasting with its unique and attractive bill pattern. However, it loses this feature in the non-breeding season, when the plumage becomes plainer. It is only a locally common bird in Ecuador, and is mainly seen on lakes and ponds in the western lowlands, although it also occurs on a few lakes in the highlands.

Least Grebe *Tachibaptus dominicus* 23cm

Vaughan Ashby

As its name indicates, this is by far the smallest of the three species of grebe that occur in Ecuador. It is only a locally common bird because of its dependence on particular wet habitats. These are usually freshwater ponds in the western lowlands, although it has also been recorded in the eastern lowlands. Like other grebe species, it builds a floating nest and the parents often carry their tiny, striped chicks on their backs. The adults are delightful, characterized by their blackish plumage, particularly on the head, which contrasts with the bright yellow eyes.

13

Waved Albatross *Diomedea irrorata*
85–93cm; Wingspan 230–240cm

birdholidays.co.uk

Also known as the Galapagos Albatross, this is the only albatross breeding close to the equator on the island of Española. However, a small population also breeds on the Isla de la Plata, just off the mainland coast and part of Ecuador's Machalilla National Park. This is much more accessible than the Galapagos Islands. Due to the relatively calm conditions at the equator, this is often seen as a rather lumbering bird, given its size and weight. It rarely enjoys the opportunity to soar and shear like its relatives of the southern ocean. Like other albatrosses, it pairs for life and is characterized by its very large, yellowish bill.

Audubon's Shearwater *Puffinus iherminieri* 27–33cm

birdholidays.co.uk

The only species of shearwater breeding on the Galapagos Islands, Audubon's Shearwater is considerably smaller and much more common than the other species that pass through the area as migrants. It is a fast-flying little seabird with gleaming white underparts and warm dark brown upperparts, which can appear black in poor light. As the birds 'shear' from side to side they appear to flash from black to white in rapid succession. It is estimated that about 10,000 pairs of this species may breed on the islands, nesting underground in burrows or crevices. The most common migrant shearwater is the Sooty Shearwater, *P. griseus*, which passes the region in the austral autumn while heading for the north Pacific, even reaching the Bering Sea during the boreal summer.

Elliot's Storm-Petrel *Oceanites gracilis* 15-16cm

birdholidays.co.uk

This is the smallest of the storm-petrel species that occur in Galapagos waters. Only three species breed on the islands, the others being vagrants or very occasional visitors. The birds nesting here are a subspecies endemic to the archipelago (unsurprisingly called *O. g. galapagoensis*). Although the population is thought to run to many thousands, its nesting colonies have not as yet been located (2007). In flight the bird is short-winged and short-tailed, with its feet protruding beyond the tail. It 'dances' on the surface much like Wilson's Storm-Petrel, *O. oceanicus*, which has also been recorded in waters off the southern mainland of Ecuador, but surely occurs in the waters surrounding Galapagos during the austral winter.

Madeiran Storm-Petrel *Oceanodroma castro* 19-21cm

birdholidays.co.uk

Breeding on the Galapagos Islands, this is one of the storm-petrel species that have been recorded in Ecuadorian waters. Also known as the Band-rumped Storm-Petrel, it has a worldwide distribution. It nests in burrows or crevices in scattered colonies on various islands and visits its nest at night. The population is thought to be about 15,000 pairs. This species does not follow ships and will usually be seen in a buoyant 'swinging' or zigzagging flight, sometimes 'shearing' in the manner of a shearwater. Its flight pattern is dependent on the wind conditions and, as a rule, the windier it is, the higher and faster the bird will 'shear'.

15

Wedge-rumped (Galapagos) Storm-Petrel
Oceanodroma tethys 18-20cm

The third of the storm-petrel species that breed on the Galapagos Islands, this is intermediate in size between the others. It is considerably easier to identify due to the extensive area of white on the rump reaching nearly to the tip of the tail. It feeds by pattering on the surface like Elliot's Storm-Petrel, *O. gracilis*, but also zigzags rapidly high over the waves, particularly in windy conditions. Unusually for a storm-petrel, this species will visit its nest during the day, thus risking attack from diurnal predators. Most storm-petrels are strictly nocturnal while visiting their nests. The population is estimated at about 200,000 pairs, but located only in a few colonies, thus suggesting that 'safety in numbers' is these birds' strategy for survival.

Galapagos Flightless Cormorant
Phalacrocorax harrisi 89-100cm

This is one of the Galapagos Islands' rarest and most enigmatic seabirds, and the only one other than the Galapagos Penguin, *Spheniscus mendiculus*, that is flightless. It is also the only extant member of the cormorant family that does not have the ability to fly. The male is larger than the female and the young birds are a glossy black. This unique species is uncommon and localized, with a total population estimated at no more than about 800 pairs. The birds nest on rocky ledges close to the high-water line and thus are very vulnerable to storms or El Niño manifestations, which seem to be becoming increasingly frequent. There are therefore considerable concerns for the future survival of this species.

Neotropic Cormorant *Phalacrocorax brasilianus* 58-73cm

This is one of the most common aquatic birds along the rivers of both the eastern and western lowlands, but it also occurs along the coast. It is also known as the Olivaceous Cormorant, and the adults do indeeed have a deep greenish-brown hue, although they appear generally blackish under normal conditions. It can be confused in its inland range with the Anhinga, *Anhinga anhinga*, but that bird has a much longer neck and bill, with pale upper wings. It also swims with most of its body submerged; the cormorant swims with its body higher in the water. It sometimes flocks to feed in particularly good fishing spots along Ecuador's lowland rivers.

Anhinga *Anhinga anhinga* 81-91cm

This close relative of the Neotropic Cormorant, *Phalacrocorax brasilianus*, is characterized by its very long, thin neck and dagger-like bill. When fishing this is all that can be seen of the bird. This particular feature is of course due to the fact that its mode of fishing is to spear its prey. The bird occurs locally along the lowland rivers and lakes on both sides of the Andes and can often be seen perched in treetops with its wings spread. The adults have a lovely silvery pattern across the upper wings and a whitish belly. The male has a black head, neck and breast. In the female this coloration is replaced by pale buffish-brown. Anhingas can sometimes be seen soaring to extreme heights, presenting a strange profile of long tail, long wings and long neck.

Blue-footed Booby *Sula nebouxii* 76–86cm

A population of this species estimated at about 10,000 pairs breeds on the Galapagos Islands, and it also breeds on Isla de la Plata, lying off the coast of Ecuador. It is quite common in the inshore waters off the coast of mainland Ecuador, where it is often seen fishing. Its main feature is its remarkable blue feet, which are used to extraordinary effect in display, although they are rather difficult to see when in flight. The bird can be confused with the much rarer Peruvian Booby, *S. variegata*, which occasionally occurs off the southern mainland coast. However, that species has a pure white head in adult plumage whereas the Blue-footed Booby has a browner, finely streaked head. Peruvian Boobies are only sporadic visitors to Ecuadorian waters and their presence often depends upon an El Niño occurrence.

Red-footed Booby *Sula sula* 66–77cm

This slim, elegant bird breeds in enormous numbers on the Galapagos Islands, where it is by far the most common species of booby, with a population estimated at about a quarter of a million pairs. There are two colour morphs – one white and the other brown. Ninety-five per cent of the birds on the Galapagos Islands are brown morphs. Intermediates also occur. The endemic subspecies *S. s. websteri*, which nests here, differs from all other populations by having a black rather than white tail. It typically nests in trees or in low shrubbery where there are no trees proper. A few pairs nest on Isla de la Plata, off mainland Ecuador. This species tends to forage far offshore.

Nazca Booby *Sula granti* 80-86cm

This booby was formerly considered a subspecies of the Masked Booby, *S. dactylatra*, which is very similar but has a green-yellow bill. The Nazca Booby has an orange-yellow bill. It breeds on the Galapagos Islands, where its population is estimated at about 10,000. Smaller numbers breed on the Isla de la Plata, just off the mainland coast. This is another expert fisherman – it often accompanies ships, riding in the slipstreams and catching flying-fish in the air as they are flushed from the sea by the vessels. Easily recognized by its white body plumage and contrasting black on the wings, it is quite unlike both the Peruvian and Blue-footed Boobies, *S. variegata* and *S. nebouxii*, which have brown upperparts.

Red-billed Tropicbird *Phaethon aethereus* 90-105cm

birdholidays.co.uk

This elegant seabird is a common breeding species on the Galapagos Islands. It breeds in scattered colonies throughout the archipelago, and is pelagic when not at the nest, foraging far offshore. Its mainly white body, red bill, black wing-tips and exceptionally long, white tail make it very distinctive and easily recognizable. This is very much a tropical seabird but it will naturally take advantage of the rich pickings of the cold Humboldt current, only occasionally being seen off the mainland coast. It has a spectacular 'meeting and greeting' ritual display in which a pair flies in tandem, with the birds mimicking each other in beautiful synchrony, their elongate tails waving behind.

Magnificent Frigatebird *Fregata magnificens* 106cm

Male   Female

This large and very distinctive bird is common along the Ecuadorian coast, where it breeds and roosts in mangroves – a habitat under serious threat in Ecuador. A predatory species with a long, hooked bill, the Magnificent Frigatebird has a very unique profile, with long, pointed wings with a span of more than 2.5m and a long, forked tail. The female has a white neck and breast. The male has a bright red, inflatable sack on his throat. This species often attacks other seabirds to make them regurgitate their last meal. It also swoops down to pick food from the water's surface, but does not land on the water. Unless breeding or roosting in trees at night, it spends nearly its entire time in the air. At times it soars to amazing heights at which it is barely visible. About 1,000 pairs nest on the Galapagos Islands.

Brown Pelican *Pelecanus occidentalis* 117-135cm

As Edward Lear famously wrote, 'A curious bird is the pelican, for its beak can hold more than its belly can'. In fact, pelicans swallow their catch straightaway. This huge, conspicuous bird of the Ecuadorian coast is ever present where a meal of fish is in the offing. It only breeds on the remote Isla Santa Clara, but readily commutes long distances. The endemic subspecies *P. o. urinator* is common on the Galapagos Islands. It could only be taken for the even larger Peruvian Pelican, *P. thagus*, which occurs irregularly along the south-west coastline. Galapagos birds have become used to Common Noddies, *Anous stoliduds*, using their heads as perches!

20

Cocoi Heron *Ardea cocoi* 127cm

Also known as the White-necked Heron, this is the most common large heron along the rivers of Ecuador's eastern lowlands and the south-west. It is very tall and conspicuous, especially when its long white neck is extended. The adults are beautiful, with a neat black cap. Their upperparts are blue-grey and their underparts a combination of black and white, the black belly contrasting sharply with the white breast. Young birds are more uniform grey, lacking the distinctive

Phil Palmer

white neck of the adults. The birds appear very large in flight, having expansive wings and an elegant, slow-flapping flight action.

Great Egret *Ardea alba* 96cm

This is the large white heron that occurs commonly in wet habitats in the lowlands on both sides of the Andes. Being typically opportunistic, it is quite commonly seen in many wet agricultural areas and even wet places within urban areas. It sometimes gathers in large numbers to take advantage of particular feeding opportunities, often with other members of the family. As is also typical of herons, it nests colonially in trees. This is a very characteristic member of the avian community because of its large size, pure white colouring and very long neck and bill. When flying it has a lazy and graceful flight action.

Snowy Egret *Egretta thula* 58cm

This common but much smaller relative of the Great Egret, *Ardea alba*, is one of no less than 21 species of the heron family that have been recorded in Ecuador. Like its larger cousin, it occurs in both North and South America and in Ecuador, in the lowlands on both sides of the Andes. It is also pure white in colour but, as it has a much smaller bill, it tends to fish for smaller prey items. This species can sometimes be confused with immature-plumaged Little Blue Herons, *E. caerulea*, which are also pure white, although they have uniformly greenish legs – Snowy Egrets have distinctive blackish legs and bright yellow feet. When in breeding plumage the birds display long white plumes on the head, as well as typical 'aigrette' plumes from the back.

birdholidays.co.uk

Rufescent Tiger Heron *Tigrisoma lineatum* 70cm

Although related to the Fasciated Tiger Heron, *T. fasciatum*, this heron species is much more likely to be seen on oxbow lakes and along smaller streams in forested habitats. It is frequently only spotted when flushed, because it is quite cryptically plumaged, but at times it perches up in prominent places to catch the early morning or late evening sun. As in the Fasciated Tiger Heron, the plumage of the immature bird, with its bold buff and black, chequered pattern, is very different from that of the adult (depicted), so that immatures can easily be mistaken for a different species. The adult is a beautiful and finely vermiculated bird with a rufous neck, usually held retracted, but capable of being extended to an astonishing length.

Boat-billed Heron *Cochlearius cochlearius* 45–54cm

Adult   Immature

This scarce creature of the eastern lowlands is quite different from other herons, having a very unusual and uniquely shaped bill. This is presumably to catch rather particular prey items. It is also unusual in having no less than four different powder glands with which to clean its plumage, an adaption shared only with the American tiger herons in the subfamily Tigrisomatinae. It spends much of the daylight hours roosting in trees and emerges to forage at night, when its huge eyes undoubtedly give it an advantage. Adults can have a body plumage that is almost white. Young birds are a pale tan colour, with a black cap.

Capped Heron *Pilherodius pileatus* 51cm

This rather small, stocky heron is another that is alone in its genus, being rather different from other members of the family. It is a bird of subtle beauty, the lovely pastel shades of its plumage only being fully appreciated with good views. The pale creamy-buff neck only gently contrasts with the dove-grey upperparts. The black cap is strikingly highlighted by the bright blue facial skin, and the head is also adorned with a pair of extravagantly elongated white plumes. The bird inhabits rivers, oxbow lakes and marshes in forested and wooded areas of the eastern lowlands, and is very often solitary.

Wood Stork *Mycteria americana* 100cm

This smaller and much more common relative of the rare Jabiru, *Jabiru mycteria*, has a wingspan of over 2m and can be a danger to small aircraft, as it sometimes soars in flocks to heights of 1,000m or more. It is most easily distinguished from the Jabiru by its black wing-tips, but is only likely to be encountered with that species along the rivers of north-eastern Ecuador. Its white plumage and black wing-tips are superficially similar to those of the King Vulture, *Sarcoramphus papa*, but the bare black head and long neck are distinctive. As this is a bird of relatively open wetland habitats, it is most likely to be seen in, or flying over, the marshlands or wetter agricultural areas of the western lowlands.

Roseate Spoonbill *Platalea ajaja* 80cm

The only spoonbill species found in the Americas, this large, rather strange, pink and white water bird, with its preposterous bill and bare head, is sometimes seen along the rivers of Ecuador's eastern lowlands, but more regularly in the marshes of the southwest. It is totally unmistakable because its appearance is so unique. Although the Chilean Flamingo, *Phoenicopterus chilensis*, occurs in the same area, it is a completely different shape. Like other members of the family, this bird uses its extraordinary spoon-shaped bill to sieve small invertebrates from the water. Arguably, it has the most outlandish appearance of any of Ecuador's water birds.

Green Ibis *Mesembrinibis cayennensis* 50–58cm

Vaughan Ashby

This member of the ibis family is rather unusual in a variety of ways. It is a bird of the watery margins in the forests of the eastern lowlands, but in Ecuador it is an uncommon creature, most likely to be seen from a boat along the edge of one of the smaller rivers, perched up on an exposed dead limb perhaps, or flushed from the bank of a stream or an oxbow lake. It also tends to be crepuscular, or even nocturnal, which lends to its somewhat 'gothic' demeanour. It has an 'oily' appearance, with dull green and bronze tones to the plumage, and rather fabulous pale green legs and bill.

Galapagos Flamingo
Phoenicopterus (ruber) glyphorhynchus 120cm

Jim Walford

Being a much more colourful bird, the Galapagos Flamingo is rather different from the Chilean Flamingo, *P. chilensis*, which occurs on the southern coast of mainland Ecuador. If given full species status, this particular form would be the world's rarest flamingo, having a population of only 500 or so birds. It also differs from its close relative on the mainland in that it has pink rather than grey legs. The immatures are a somewhat 'grubby' white, recalling an 'ugly duckling' scenario, given that the adults are very beautiful. This species breeds on saline lagoons, where it is very vulnerable to disturbance.

27

Limpkin *Aramus guarauna* 66–71cm

This is a rather strange, large, long-necked and long-legged wading bird of the south-western lowlands, locally inhabiting wet habitats such as marshes and rice fields. It is unique in that it does not appear to have any close relatives, and is therefore placed in a family of its own – the Aramidae. It has a dark, spotted plumage and a long, decurved bill, which it uses to extract water snails from their shells. In the north-east it can sometimes be seen from boats along vegetated riverbanks, but it is more often found on oxbow lakes and other backwaters. When seen flying it looks quite unusual, resembling a large, somewhat ungainly ibis, but it has a very different, 'jerky' flight action.

Horned Screamer *Anhima cornuta* 90cm

One of three species in a family of strange birds that look like a cross between a goose and a raptor, this bird forages in wet habitats and perches conspicuously on the tops of trees. It is a very large inhabitant of Ecuador's eastern lowland rainforests, where it is uncommon and local. In the west it is now very rare, but it may be seen on oxbow lakes or riverbanks in this region. The birds have loud calls – hence their name. The horn referred to in the name is actually a single plume, which protrudes from the front of the bird's head. Remarkably for such an ungainly looking bird, it sometimes soars gracefully over the forest. More usually it is seen flapping hard to get its considerable bulk airborne.

28

Black-bellied Whistling-Duck
Dendrocygna autumnalis 50cm

This species is closely related to the Fulvous Whistling-Duck, *D. bicolor*, but is much more likely to be seen perched in trees. It is largely nocturnal, and gives its loud whistling-calls by day and night. Flocks are often seen (and heard) at dawn and dusk, as they travel between feeding and roosting places. The species can be found in any marshy place that presents feeding opportunities, including man-made habitats such as cattle-ranch drinking pools and rice fields. It displays a very obvious white bar on the wing when in flight.

Torrent Duck *Merganetta armata* 38-42cm

One of the most extraordinary members of the duck family and one of the most easily recognized, this bird is only found along Ecuador's fast-flowing montane and submontane streams and rivers. It requires unpolluted water and is quite common where these conditions exist. The male bird (depicted) has a black and white striped head, different from that of the female, which has a plainer rufous and grey pattern. The precocious ducklings can swim in the fast-flowing rivers at an early age, and may be seen negotiating rapids with clearly inherent skill.

Vaughan Ashby

29

Yellow-billed Pintail *Anas georgica* 48–56cm

Vaughan Ashby

This bird occurs principally in Páramo, at high altitudes of up to about 4,000m. Its preferred habitats consist of lakes and ponds, where it can be observed feeding by 'up-ending', with its long, pointed tail sticking up in the air as it nibbles at the aquatic vegetation below. It maintains this position by paddling – in effect 'treading water'. It also ocurs in marshy areas, where it can be seen 'dabbling' – walking forwards and sieving food from or close to the surface. Although not brightly coloured, this is an elegant and attractive duck.

White-cheeked Pintail *Anas bahamensis* 46cm

birdholidays.co.uk

This bird is locally distributed along the mainland coast but fairly common on the Galapagos Islands, where the endemic subspecies *A. b. galapagensis* is widely distributed. This subspecies (depicted) has a rather different appearance from that of the mainland form, which has more crisply contrasting white 'cheeks'. This pretty and rather delicate little duck is typical of the genus *Anas*, as it feeds by 'dabbling' and 'up-ending'. It is most easily seen on the mainland, on the lagoons of the Santa Elena Peninsula, where it sometimes congregates in large numbers.

Andean Condor *Vultur gryphus* 106cm

Vaughan Ashby

One of the largest flying birds in the world, with a wingspan of 3m or more, this is also one of the most enigmatic birds of the high Andes. It is sometimes captured for use in traditional ceremonies in rural mountain areas. Although it is not a particularly common bird in Ecuador, it can be seen in many localities along the Andean chain that runs the length of the country. Many sightings are, however, misidentifications of the much more common Black-chested Buzzard-eagle, *Geranoaetus melanoleucus*, though the condor never displays a white belly in any plumage. Young Andean Condors do not display the white collar that so obviously distinguishes the adults. Close to Quito, the birds are perhaps most easily seen at the pass at Papallacta.

King Vulture *Sarcoramphus papa* 76cm

Vaughan Ashby

Often referred to as El Condor by lowland indigenous people, this is the largest and most powerful of the lowland neotropical vultures. It utilizes the abilities of other vulture species, particularly the Greater Yellow-headed Vulture, *Cathartes melambrotus*, to literally sniff out carrion, by watching them home in on their prey and then following them down to take the greater share of the spoils. It can then be seen enjoying itself as the other vulture species stand around waiting for it to leave (that is if it can even get off the ground by the time it has finished its meal). Its large size, multi-coloured head and mostly white body plumage set it apart from all other New World vultures.

31

Black Vulture *Coragyps atratus* 63cm

Vaughan Ashby

This is the most common sedentary member of the family and the vulture most likely to be seen scavenging in urban areas. It is often allowed to do so undisturbed, especially in areas where there is no other refuse collection service! It is different in general appearance from other vultures and thus is easily recognized – it has a wrinkly black head and a somewhat ungainly flight on short wings, as opposed to the lovely tilting and swooping flight of the Turkey Vulture, *Cathartes aura*. It is quite voracious and can run fast on the ground and successfully fight for spoils with other vulture species, often simply overwhelming them by sheer numbers. A flock of Black Vultures in action can be a rather unpleasant spectacle.

Greater Yellow-headed Vulture
Cathartes melambrotus 75-80cm

This vulture is very typical of Ecuador's lowland eastern rainforests, where it is the most common vulture soaring above the trees. It closely resembles the Turkey Vulture, *C. aura*, but is somewhat broader winged and has dark inner primaries. The most interesting feature of this bird is probably its ability to locate carrion in dense forest with its extraordinary sense of smell – which is perhaps the most acute of any bird in the world. Other vultures watch and follow it, as it has the greater olfactory capability, then home in on the food source and compete with this species.

Turkey Vulture *Cathartes aura* 66-75cm

One of the most ubiquitous large birds to be seen in the skies over Ecuador, the Turkey Vulture is often mistaken for a condor or eagle. It is identifiable by its quite distinctive profile in flight, black plumage and, at close range, variably coloured head. Two different populations occur in Ecuador, one native and the other composed of migrants from North America. The bird has a graceful, lilting flight on long wings, as opposed to the short wings of the Black Vulture. It is very similar in appearance to the Greater Yellow-headed Vulture, *C. melambrotus*, of the lowland eastern forests, but is always recognizable by its multicoloured yellow, purple and pink head and its presence over urban areas.

Galapagos Hawk *Buteo galapagoensis* 55cm

This endemic hawk's population has declined markedly in recent years and its status is now officially regarded as Vulnerable. It is currently (2008) thought to number only a few hundred birds. The only resident diurnal raptor on the Galapagos Islands, it is both a hunter and a scavenger – and the scourge of some of the breeding seabirds, taking many of their eggs and young. It is only likely to be confused with the Osprey, *Pandion haliaetus*, which is a rare visitor to the islands, but the Galapagos Hawk never displays the white crown and underparts of that species. It is a dark blackish-brown bird with paler flight feathers. The young birds are typically more mottled and streaked than the adults.

birdholidays.co.uk

Roadside Hawk *Buteo magnirostris* 38cm

This is one of the most commonly encountered raptors in Ecuador, frequently seen in cleared areas, particularly at roadsides, as suggested by its very apt common name. In some places it would be better known as the 'Riverside Hawk', because it is regularly seen from boats when perched up in riverside trees. It has a very distinctive, rather inelegant, flappy flight action due to its short wings, which also display an obvious rufous patch in the primaries. The adults are grey-brown above and barred on the breast and belly, while the immatures (depicted) are browner. The bird's distinctive mewing call is commonly heard where it occurs.

Mangrove Black Hawk *Buteogallus subtilis* 39–47cm

This is a bird that is largely restricted to mangroves, and in this respect it can be separated from the larger but similar Great Black Hawk, *B. urubitinga*, with which it does not generally share this habitat. The tail pattern is the main plumage feature that distinguishes this species from its relative – the black basal part of the tail gives the bird the appearance of having a narrower white band. It is restricted to its 'niche' habitat due to the fact that it feeds largely on crabs.

Vaughan Ashby

Zone-tailed Hawk *Buteo albonotatus* 50cm

This long-winged and elegant black hawk from both the forests of the lowlands and the foothills of the Andes is a bird that causes some confusion as it bears a rather unlikely and unusual resemblance to the Turkey Vulture, *Cathartes aura*. Its dark colouration and habit of cruising on uplifted wings, with frequent tilting, like the vulture, is the cause of this confusion. However, with a good view, you can see its banded (zoned) tail, finely barred flight feathers and yellow area of bare skin at the base of the bill, which is known in raptors as the cere. It is quite an uncommon bird but is almost certainly overlooked because it is often mistaken for the much more common but larger Turkey Vulture.

Black-chested Buzzard-eagle
Geranoaetus melanoleucus 68cm

birdholidays.co.uk

This large, distinctive raptor is generally easy to identify as there are no other similar raptors in its range. In fact, it is an unmistakable bird given its extraordinary shape and easily recognizable pattern below. It has very broad wings, a very short tail and a characteristic light belly and contrasting dark breast. It is an extremely large raptor that is quite obvious in the air, as it tends to cover ground quite slowly when hunting, often hovering in one position for a long time. Its preys consists largely of small mammals. This is a bird of the high Andes, and its impressive size can mistakenly lead to it being identified as a condor.

Black Hawk-Eagle *Spizaetus tyrannus* 63–72cm

This beautiful, graceful raptor from forested habitats of the lowlands and foothills of Ecuador often betrays its presence by its loud calls. These are usualy a far-carrying yelping, perhaps '*wip wip weeeeeeer*', which is generally uttered in flight while soaring above its forested domain. The bird has a long tail and a distinctive outline, characteristic of the *Spizaetus* genus of hawk-eagles, produced by the bulging rear edge of the wing and pronounced by the 'pinched-in' effect of the very innermost secondaries. Being largely black, it can often appear to be a sillhouette. Better views reveal an attractive and intricate chequered pattern across all the flight feathers.

Eustace Barnes

Harpy Eagle *Harpia harpyja* 86–94cm

Being an iconic bird of prey and the largest, most powerful raptor in Ecuador, this is one of the most sought-after species by birders. A huge bill and talons enable this eagle to take large prey such as monkeys and sloths. The adult looks quite similar to the very rare Crested Eagle, *Morphnus guianensis*, but that species is smaller and less powerful. Harpy Eagles inhabit areas of lowland forest that are able to support the quite large animals that they prey on. They are highly revered by indigenous people, but unfortunately are sometimes captured and kept as symbols of power. A pair will rear only a single chick once, over a two-year period. The young birds have white heads and thus look very different from the adults.

36

Swallow-tailed Kite *Elanoides forficatus* 60cm

This elegant raptor with long, pointed wings is one of the most conspicuous and loveliest birds of prey in Ecuador. It is instantly recognizable, with its long, forked white tail, grey and black upper wings, gleaming white head and underparts, and striking black and white underwing pattern. There are both resident populations and migrants that visit particular areas seasonally. The birds are nearly always seen soaring over the forest, swooping down and picking small prey from the canopy foliage while in flight, and often occur in flocks.

Snail Kite *Rostrhamus sociabilis* 36-45cm

This highly specialized bird of the kite family has a bill that is specifically designed to deal with the freshwater snails that are its sole food source. It is found around the marshy areas, rice fields and waterways of Ecuador's lowland south-west. It can be quite common where these wetland habitats exist, and may be seen flying in the usual 'floating' kite fashion over these areas, where it finds its very particular prey. Typical of the kite family, it is a beautiful and elegant bird. However, the adult, with its uniform dark grey plumage and black and white banded tail, is considerably different from the immature bird, which is brown above and streaked below.

Lined Forest Falcon *Micrastur gilvicollis* 32-37cm

A denizen of the lowland Amazon forest, this falcon is rarely seen but quite often heard calling at dawn and dusk, as it seems to be semi-nocturnal or crepuscular. All the forest falcons have a distinctive yelping call but are rarely heard calling during the day. This behaviour is very typical for this family of rainforest-dwelling raptors, and is often the only indication that forest falcons are present at all. Like Ecuador's other five forest falcon species, and as its name suggests, this bird is an adept forest hunter with the agility to skilfully negotiate the dark understorey at high speed. It hunts many birds and, as its large white eyes attest, can do so in the low light conditions of the sometimes almost closed tree canopy.

Carunculated Caracara
Phalcoboenus carunculatus 51-56cm

A very different bird from the Black and Red-throated Caracaras, *Daptrius ater* and *Ibycter americanus*, of the lowlands, both in appearance and since it is strictly a bird of the high Andes, this species is most often seen soaring on long, stiff wings or striding around purposefully on open ground. In adult plumage it is a striking raptor with contrasting black and white plumage. It is somewhat locally dispersed, but is very conspicuous in the open Páramo habitat in which it is found. It is most similar to the Mountain Caracara, *P. megalopterus*, which occurs to the south in similar habitats. However, the Mountain Caracara has a solid black throat and breast. It is possible that both species could be encountered together in the mountains around Loja, in the south of Ecuador.

birdholidays.co.uk

Bat Falcon *Falco rufigularis* 25cm

This very attractive little falcon is
quite a common bird of the lowlands on both sides of the Andes.
In the east of Ecuador, it generally prefers areas close to water, so
it is most often seen along the
rivers and oxbow lakes of the
region. Its plumage is very similar to that of the Orange-breasted
Falcon, *F. deiroleucus*, but that
species is considerably larger and
much rarer. Care must be taken
not to confuse a large female Bat
Falcon with a small male of that
species. Bat Falcons, as their
name suggests, are partial to bats,
and are therefore rather crepuscular in their habits, spending
much of the day sitting quietly on
dead trees. However, they are
very fast in flight and will also
hunt other birds, particularly
swallows and martins. They are

Dave Willis

very dashing, both in appearance and style, and have the most
beautiful plumage pattern, with a black head, white collar, rufous
belly and black-barred breast.

Spix's Guan *Penelope jacquacu* 76-84cm

Vaughan Ashby

This large guan is a bird of the lowland forest of eastern Ecuador
and often skulks in vine tangles in the lower levels, where it remains
hidden until flushed. When it is surprised like this it can explode
from cover, making a great deal of commotion, which can be quite
startling. Although generally quite a vocal creature, it spends long
periods without calling. It can only be seen perched higher or in
the open in early morning or late evening. It is generally fairly common, but is usually absent from forest areas within walking distance from human habitation.

Common Piping Guan *Pipile pipile* 68-73cm

Phil Palmer

Another bird of Ecuador's eastern lowland forests, this species is unmistakable with its strange shaggy crest and blue dewlap. It is also known as the White-winged Piping Guan. Like the Spix's Guan, *Penelope jacquacu*, it is almost always absent from areas close to towns and villages, and is quite common where it is protected or lives in more remote areas. Very much an arboreal creature, it is able to run and jump along tree limbs and move through the tree-tops with some grace. It can be quite tame where it is not threatened. When in flight, it configures its primary flight feathers so that they vibrate in the air stream, producing a strange and distinctive rattling or whirring sound, which reverberates through the forest. The 'piping' relates to the bird's piercing, whistling calls.

Dark-backed Wood Quail
Odontophorus melanotus 23-25cm

This species is typical of the wood quails in its behaviour, but it is the plainest of a family of birds with generally cryptic plumage. It is a bird of the forested subtropical slopes of north-western Ecuador. As is usual of birds in this family, it wanders the forest floor and unless flushed is unlikely to be seen, as it is unobtrusive and furtive. If you are lucky a bird

Eustace Barnes

may run a short distance and freeze, relying on its camouflage to conceal its presence – this species depends on its dark, plain plumage to blend with the shadows of the dark understorey and leaf litter of the forest floor. It is far more often heard than seen, especially in the late evening, when its calls echo around the forest and are designed to be heard from a long distance.

40

Plumbeous Rail *Pardirallus sanguinolentus* 27cm

This bird is rather local in wet habitats in Loja. It is quite conspicuous for a rail, as it spends a considerable amount of time foraging in open marshy habitats. Slaty-grey below and dark brown above, it has a slender pale-green bill with red and blue spots at the base, and red legs, making it a very handsome bird and rather elegant compared to its near relative the Common Moorhen, *Gallinula chloropus*, with which it often shares its habitat. It is replaced in the foothills of the eastern Andes by the closely related and very similar Blackish Rail, *P. nigricans*. That species has a darker bill lacking the red spot, and also a whitish throat, which this species does not have.

Grey-necked Wood-Rail *Aramides cajanea* 39cm

birdholidays.co.uk

This large and rather lovely rail is usually a fairly common bird where it occurs in the lowlands of the east. Unlike many members of the rail family, it is relatively unafraid of venturing into the open, particularly in the twilight hours. However, it is still a wary creature, and will often be seen scuttling into nearby cover. One of four species of wood-rail found in Ecuador, it is probably seen more often than the others as it is large and conspicuous. It may be seen in a variety of marshy habitats and usually prefers places with at least some forest cover. It is very vocal early in the morning and in the late evening – its loud vocalizations are often given in an antiphonal duet and can sound quite frenzied.

Sungrebe *Heliornis fulica* 30cm

A member of the finfoot family, of which there are only three species, this is the smallest, and the only one in the New World. When in the water swimming, it superficially resembles a grebe but has a very different bill, and there are no grebes that have a similar striped pattern on the head in adult plumage, although young grebes are usually striped. A secretive and attractive aquatic bird of the lowland rainforests, it has a neat black and white striped head, and is plain brown above and white below. It usually stays close to the banks of rivers and oxbow lakes, and is often seen swimming under overhanging vegetation. Unlike grebes, this species can walk on land, like the other finfoots, and is also able to climb up into trees.

Sunbittern *Eurypyga helias* 50cm

In a family of its own, this is one of the most amazing birds of Ecuador. It is an extraordinarily cryptically plumaged bird, with a fantastic display to deter predators. This involves opening the wings and flashing eye-like markings, which makes it look more like a giant moth than a bird. Its complicated plumage pattern also allows it to remain inconspicuous in open environments, blending with its surroundings, especially when on a stony river beach lacking any vegetation at all. It frequents streams of the lower east and west Andean slopes, and also oxbow lakes of the eastern lowlands, where it feeds on various aquatic creatures and stealthily hunts butterflies along the riverbanks. It is a truly enigmatic and very spectacular bird.

Grey-winged Trumpeter *Psophia crepitans* 46-52cm

Jim Walford

This truly magnificent, though elusive and enigmatic bird, is always a joy to see, but is rarely encountered unless you spend many hours walking the trails through the lowland forest that is its home. The birds themselves also spend many hours walking in the forest. Known locally in Ecuador as the Trompetero, the Grey-winted Trumpeter is widely hunted. Due to the various loud alarm calls it makes when disturbed, it is sometimes trapped and kept as a pet or 'guard bird' by people living in the forests of the eastern lowlands. It is frequently active at night, when its low-frequency, tremulous calls are sometimes the only clue to its presence. However, these sounds travel far through the forest so its proximity is hard to judge.

Wattled Jacana *Jacana jacana* 25 cm

Vaughan Ashby

This bird is also known as the 'lily trotter' due to its ability to walk on aquatic vegetation like lily pads. It does this by utilizing its very long toes, which spread its weight. It has long, thin legs, large red facial wattles, rich deep chestnut upperparts and a blackish body plumage, which lends to its general attractive appearance. The bird's quite startling, distinctive yellow wing feathers can be seen when it takes flight. Immature birds are white below. This is a relatively common species in marshy habitats on both sides of the Andes.

Rufous-bellied Seedsnipe *Attagis gayi* 30 cm

Eustace Barnes

This member of a rather strange family of South American ground-dwelling birds that reach their northern geographical limit in Ecuador is a bird of the higher scree slopes of the volcanos that characterize the Ecuadorian highlands, often close to the snowline. It is a beautiful and cryptically plumaged creature that is often elusive as it occurs in low densities in this harsh environment. It is also perfectly camouflaged in this stony terrain. Once located it may be quite tame, and with care and stealth may allow a remarkably close approach. However, if flushed, a group may fly a long distance and be extremely difficult to re-locate. This is an enigmatic bird of the most extreme environment in Ecuador.

Wilson's Phalarope *Phalaropus tricolor* 22-24cm

Vaughan Ashby

This long-distance migrant from North America is quite common in the northern winter months, both on Ecuador's coastal lagoons and lakes at high altitude, and on the Galapagos Islands. It is sometimes seen in large flocks, which may pick along the shore or swim and spin to stir up prey from the muddy bottom. Although totally different in appearance between its summer and winter plumage, it is always recognizable by its needle-thin bill. The name 'tricolor' relates to its exquisite summer plumage. Birds in this plumage may be seen in Ecuador in March, passing through en route to their Canadian breeding grounds. However, this species is more often seen wearing its grey and white winter dress.

44

Solitary Sandpiper *Tringa solitaria* 21cm

Jim Walford

A common migrant to mainland Ecuador from its North American breeding grounds during the northern winter, this species thus tends to occur in the country mainly between September and March. It is also an occasional migrant, in small numbers, to the Galapagos Islands during this period. It is nearly always seen on freshwater pools inland and is very often alone (hence its name). Although it is similar to the larger Lesser Yellowlegs, *T. flavipes*, with which it may often be seen, it is a much slimmer and more delicate bird. It also has shorter and somewhat greener legs than that species, and is darker and less spangled.

Wandering Tattler *Heteroscelus incanus* 26–29cm

brdholidays.co.uk

This shore bird from the Arctic tundra is a scarce visitor to rocky shores of the mainland coast, but a regular visitor to the Galapagos Islands during the northern winter months and a common passage migrant en route to winter quarters as far south as New Zealand. A truly global wanderer, it is a shore bird that prefers to probe into rock crevices rather than to forage along the sandier shoreline, and it is most likely to be seen alone or in small groups, rather than flocks. Often seen in the company of turnstones, or surfbirds, the Wandering Tattler is truly one of the great migrants of the planet, here one day and gone the next, perhaps to make its next landfall thousands of miles away.

Whimbrel *Numenius phaeopus* 43cm

Vaughan Ashby

This large shore bird is a very long-distance migrant that breeds on the tundras of the Arctic and is a common migrant to the shores of the Ecuadorian coast during the northern winter months, mainly in October to April. A member of the curlew family, it is characterized by its curved bill and striped head, but it is typical of curlews with its brown, streaky and camouflaged general pattern. This is designed to protect the birds on their breeding grounds – unlike most shore birds they keep the same plumage in the non-breeding season. The curved bill is used to probe for prey in mud and other soft marshy habitats. The bird's call is very distinctive – a quick succession of seven whistles. It is a regular visitor to the Galapagos Islands.

Andean Snipe *Gallinago jamesoni* 28-30cm

birdholidays.co.uk

Although snipes are described as 'shore birds' in some publications, this species of snipe will never be seen on a shore. The Andean Snipe is a bird of the high Páramo, up to about 4,400m altitude. It is a large, stocky snipe, which is only likely to be seen well if flushed and then carefully tracked down and located on the ground. It is most active in the twilight hours of dusk and dawn, and is therefore a hard target for birders. Its '*wikko...wikko... wikko...*' calls may be heard in the half-light, as it performs its aerial display over the high mountain slopes. However, even seeing it in the air is a challenge because it stops displaying in the morning, when it gets light.

Ruddy Turnstone *Arenaria interpres* 23cm

birdholidays.co.uk

Although this is a bird that breeds on the Arctic tundra, it visits Ecuador during the northern winter and can be found anywhere along the coast, sometimes in large numbers. It is also a common migrant visitor to the Galapagos Islands and, like many other North American shore birds, is usually present in September to March, although young birds are often present all year round. As its name suggests, it is generally to be found foraging on rocky shores, typically turning over stones and seaweed in search of prey. However, unlike most migrant shore birds, it is exceptionally opportunistic – this photograph was taken in a beachside restaurant, where the birds were feeding on peanuts, sometimes even on the bar top! The author has also seen them feeding on discarded picnic sandwiches and even scavenging on dead birds on the shore.

Andean Lapwing *Vanellus resplendens* 33cm

birdholidays.co.uk

One of the most conspicuous and noisy birds of the high Andes, this species is often found in irrigated areas close to human habitation, but also in more remote marshy or damp grassy areas. It is a rather common bird and has a very distinctive, mostly green and grey plumage pattern. A typical member of the *Vanellus* genus, with its loud alarm calls and striking plumage, it also has vivid red eyes. As its name suggests, it is common at high altitudes, occurring in suitable habitats at up to 4,500m. However, like many birds of the highest elevations in the Andes of Ecuador, it occasionally comes down to lower elevations, especially when conditions are particularly severe at the high altitudes.

47

Baird's Sandpiper *Calidris bairdii* 18cm

Vaughan Ashby

This bird migrates through Ecuador in variable numbers, heading south from its breeding areas in the Canadian Arctic during the boreal autumn and back north again in March–April. However, unlike the other members of the family, this is a species that is most often seen in the highlands. Most birds spend the northern winter further south, and this species has one of the longest migrations of all American birds. It is an elegant, long-winged member of the *Calidris* sandpiper genus. This is one of the most characteristic features of the bird – these little sandpipers, or 'peeps', are very similar to each other and sometimes difficult to identify.

Western Sandpiper *Calidris mauri* 15-16cm

Vaughan Ashby

Unlike the previous species, this little sandpiper is very much a bird of the coast, especially where there are mudflats on which it forages. It is not usually found inland, except when forced to wait out very high tides. It is very similar to the Semi-palmated Sandpiper, *C. pusilla*, with which it mixes frequently during its stay in Ecuador, sometimes in very large numbers. The Western Sandpiper has a rather longer bill than its close relative, but it can be very difficult to differentiate between them when they are in their winter plumage. Another tiny 'peep' is the Least Sandpiper, *C. minutilla*, which visits at the same time (usually only in August–April), but that species often occurs in freshwater habitats.

Royal Tern *Thalasseus maximus* 49cm

Vaughan Ashby

This large member of the tern family is regularly seen along the Ecuadorian coast and on the Galapagos Islands, usually during the northern winter months. Unlike the Large-billed Tern, *Phaetusa simplex*, it does not occur inland or over fresh water. In breeding plumage it has a solid black cap, but it is usually seen in its winter dress, when its forehead is white and its bill is orange-yellow. It fishes in bays in particular, and this is where it is most easily seen. It also fishes far out at sea when the opportunity arises to exploit a shoal near the surface, and can often be seen being hounded by Magnificent Frigatebirds, *Fregata magnificens*.

Common Noddy *Anous stolidus* 38-45cm

birdholidays.co.uk

This is a breeding bird of the Galapagos Islands that is apparently unrecorded in the waters off mainland Ecuador as yet (2008). Common Noddies commonly use pelicans' heads as perches (depicted). The pelican stirs up titbits, which the noddy then scavenges. This noddy is a common resident, breeding in small colonies throughout the archipelago. It is characterized by its all-dark plumage and lovely white cap. The young bird in its first full plumage lacks this feature. The noddies differ from terns in the genus *Sterna* in that they do not dive for prey but pick it up from the water's surface.

Yellow-billed Tern *Sterna superciliaris* 23-25cm

This beautiful little tern is a common bird along the larger rivers in the eastern lowlands of Ecuador, where it breeds on the exposed sandbars during the dry season. It hovers with rapid wingbeats and plunge dives for small fish. It also frequently fishes in the numerous oxbow lakes of the region. Given its very small size, it is unlikely to be confused with any other tern within its Amazonian range. Its small yellow bill is diagnostic. Outside the breeding season, its crisp black cap becomes mottled and indistinct and its forehead turns white. Two other similar-sized small terns sometimes occur on the coast: the Peruvian Tern, *S. lorata*, from the south, and the Least Tern, *S. antillarum*, a rare migrant from North America.

Large-billed Tern *Phaetusa simplex* 38cm

With its massive yellow bill, this large tern is very distinctive, and is an obvious, common and easily recognized bird of the Amazonian lowland river systems and oxbow lakes. Unlike most terns, it does not usually occur in coastal waters, being normally a freshwater species. It is often found nesting on sandbanks alongside Black Skimmers, *Rynchops niger*. The extremely striking pattern on its upper wings, comprising three triangular areas of black, white and grey, is very noticeable. It commonly follows boats travelling along lowland rivers as they churn up prey from the normally muddy and murky waters.

50

Black Skimmer *Rynchops niger* 45cm

This extraordinary bird is quite uncommon along the lowland rivers east of the Andes, but more regular on lagoons along the coast, particularly those at Salinas on the Santa Elena Peninsula. It is one of three species in the world that are unique in that they feed by flying just above the surface of the river with the lower mandible in the water, snapping up prey items as they go along. Skimmers have the unique adaptation of having the lower mandible considerably longer than the upper one to enable them to perform this spectacular feeding feat. This is one of the most easily recognized birds along the rivers, with its strange red and black bill and black and white plumage, and with the prominent white trailing edge to its long, pointed wings.

Franklin's Gull *Larus pipixcan* 35cm

During the northern winter months this pretty gull migrates from the Canadian prairies and follows the Pacific coast, usually passing through Ecuadorian waters in October or early November. It will therefore generally be seen in its winter plumage, which lacks the black head of its breeding plumage. In adult plumage, it is characterized by its obvious black wing-tips with contrasting white spots, which are known in gulls as mirrors. The Laughing Gull, *L. atricilla*, is a much more common wintering species in Ecuador.

51

Swallow-tailed Gull *Creagrus furcatus* 50cm

One of the most beautiful members of the gull family, this species is an endemic breeding bird of the Galapagos Islands. It is quite a large, rather strange-looking gull that has a striking wing pattern, with large white patches and mostly black outer flight feathers. As its name suggests, it also has a pronounced forked white tail, which in the immature has a black band at the tip. The species has very large eyes, which give a clue to its largely nocturnal lifestyle. In the non-breeding season, it can be seen off the South American coast as far south as Chilean waters, but always offshore and never coming to land during the time it spends away from the islands.

Andean Gull *Larus serranus* 46–48cm

The archetypal gull of the high Andes, this species breeds in high-altitude bogs and, as is typical of the family, can be seen in any place where an opportunity of a meal arises. It is probably most often seen foraging in pasture and ploughed fields, and around wetland edges, but the town dump is as good a place as any to see it. It nests in small colonies, often in very isolated and exposed places, and can be seen flying high over the mountains, especially during the summer months when feeding its chicks. It does not range into the lowlands outside the breeding season, even in cold weather, but will descend to lower, more temperate levels within its montane range. At this time, the adults lose their black hoods and show only a small dark patch on the rear of the ear coverts.

Lava Gull *Larus fuliginosus* 51-55cm

birdholidays.co.uk

Like the Lava Heron, *Butorides sundevalli*, this gull is aptly named and is endemic to the extraordinary group of islands that is the Galapagos. It is also rather similar to that species in respect of its dark grey plumage that blends with the colour of the rock. This lends it protection from predators such as the Galapagos Hawk, *Buteo galapagoensis*, which targets its colonies during the breeding season in search of an easy meal of a gull chick. The young are also very dark, generally an overall deep chocolate brown, with slightly paler feather edges. This is an unmistakable gull and it is also the rarest gull in the world, with less than 400 breeding pairs. It tends to spend much time scavenging along the shoreline and breeds close to the shore, often just above the tide line.

Galapagos Dove *Zenaida galapagoensis* 18-23cm

This lovely – indeed spectacular – member of the dove family is an unmistakable species, with its ornate iridescent plumage, red legs and blue eye-ring. It is found in many locations on the Galapagos Islands, where it is an endemic resident. It is quite common generally but locally less so, as on Floreana, San Cristobal and Santa Cruz. It is represented

Jim Walford

by two subspecies. The nominate form, which occurs on most islands, is replaced on Darwin and Wolf by the subspecies *Z. g. exsul*. The bird breeds during the rainy season, which is usually in February–June, and nests on the ground, secreted beneath a rock or a cactus to conceal it from predators.

Ruddy Ground-Dove *Columbina talpacoti* 18cm

Female

Male

This is one of the most attractive members of the ground-dove family, of which there are ten species in Ecuador. It is a common and obvious member of the avian community in the Amazonian lowlands, and is often flushed from roadsides and the edges of villages, gardens and various other open and marginal habitats. It is quite a tame bird and is thus often well seen. The male is distinctive, having rusty-coloured upperparts that contrast with a soft blue-grey cap and nape, and a paler, pinker underside. The female has less obvious reddish hues and somewhat resembles the Plain-breasted Ground-Dove, *C. minuta*, but she is nearly always accompanied by a male, so giving a strong clue to her identity.

Blue Ground-Dove *Claravis pretiosa* 21cm

Female

Male

This pretty member of the genus *Claravis* is generally a common bird where it occurs. This is usually inside or at the borders and clearings of forest and woodland in the lowlands on both sides of the Andes. It is quite inconspicuous in general, because it normally stays in or close to cover, rarely far from the ground. It is almost always seen in pairs or perhaps in small groups at *saltados* (salt licks or mineral licks). Its close relative, the Maroon-chested Ground-Dove, *C. mondetoura*, is a very rare and much sought-after montane species that is closely tied to stands of bamboo in the highland forests of Ecuador.

54

Eared Dove *Zenaida auriculata* 25cm

One of the most widespread doves of the region, the Eared Dove is common in both highland and lowland areas of Ecuador. It is fast flying and rather anonymous until seen well, when its subtle but attractive plumage pattern can be clearly viewed. At close range the bird is more distinctive, displaying a pretty, iridescent purple-pink neck patch and a small dark mark on each side of the head (the 'ears' that give it its name). It resembles several other dove species in having white outer tips to the tail, but has a distinctive pointed tail.

Marañón Pigeon *Columbea oenops* 33-34cm

This lovely, delicate pigeon is found only in the extreme south of the country. It is just one of the many species being added to the list of birds recorded in Ecuador as people increasingly visit the area. The lovely pastel lilac and mauve tones to the bird's plumage are characteristic. It has been confused (by the author) with the much more common and closely related Pale-vented Pigeon, but that species does occur in the same area.

Plumbeous Pigeon *Patagioenas plumbea* 30cm

This large plain pigeon is a common bird in the forests of Ecuador's eastern lowlands and the subtropical foothill forests of the western slope of the Andes. It may make visits to seasonally available food sources at up to about 2,000m elevation. The birds in the photograph are taking mineral salts from a *saltado* (mineral lick). This is a common practice of many forest birds, which rely largely on fruit in their diet. Although nutritious, some of the fruits of the forest are very acidic and the birds need to balance this by consuming naturally occurring alkalids in the clay at certain places. Parrots in particular are often to be found in such places.

Dusky-billed Parrotlet *Forpus modestus* 12cm

This tiny parrot is at the opposite end of the scale from the macaws in terms of size, being one of the smallest members of the family in Ecuador. It can be seen in groups in flowering or fruiting trees, where the birds gather in noisy congregations. Their calls are distinctive and are often the first indication of a flock of these garrulous little parrots in the area. They are often seen flying overhead in rapid flight, 'twittering' wildly as they seek out the next meal. Their longer distance movements are often seasonal and depend on food sources from fruiting trees. The birds in the photograph are licking salt from a riverside beach to aid the digestion of acidic fruits on which so many parrots rely.

White-eyed Parakeet *Aratinga leucopthalma* 32cm

The most uniformly coloured member of the *Aratinga* genus, this is a common species of the eastern lowlands and lower foothills. Its underwing displays a pattern of red and yellow, and it has variable amounts of scattered, random red markings on the sides of the neck and the nape, but otherwise it is uniform green in colour. It usually roams around locally in noisy flocks of 10–50 birds, but sometimes in larger congregations. In general, this is a common and conspicuous bird occurring in a wide range of Ecuador's wooded and semi-wooded habitats, from true forests to parks and suburban gardens.

Red-billed Parrot *Pionus sordidus* 27-29cm

The *Pionus* parrots are medium sized and short tailed. They are particularly characterized by their flight, which is very different from that of the *Amazona* species with their rather shallow wingbeats. The *Pionus* parrots fly with deep wingbeats. This particular species occurs above the lowland range of the Blue-headed Parrot, *P. menstruus*. It is a bird of the subtropical forests of the foothills of the Andes, both east and west, ranging up into the temperate zone, where the habitat can be described as cloud forest. It utters far-carrying '*keewank, keewank, keewank*' calls, and is of course typified by its red bill.

Eustace Barnes

57

Blue-headed Parrot *Pionus menstruus* 27–29 cm

Phil Palmer

Unlike the previous species, this is a bird of the lowlands on both sides of the Andes. It is often quite common and usually rather conspicuous, due to its habit of flying around calling loudly, using a far-carrying, rapidly delivered and high-pitched '*kewink, kewink. kewink...*' call. The adults have richly coloured blue heads, but the immature birds (depicted) less so. The scientific name alludes to the red undertail coverts (vent), although all the *Pionus* species display this feature. A very popular pet, this bird is often trapped by indigenous people. It will tolerate secondary habitats and disturbed areas.

Scaly-naped Amazon *Amazona mercenaria* 31–33cm

Phil Palmer

This species of parrot in the genus *Amazona* is rather unusual, because it is the only one that inhabits the higher temperate forests of Ecuador. It shares its range and habitat with the Red-billed and White-capped Parrots, *P. sordidus* and *P. seniloides*, at an elevation of about 1,200–2,600m. It is best identified by its different manner of flight, which employs shallow wingbeats rather than the deep flapping of its relatives in the *Pionus* genus. This is a local and uncommon bird in Ecuador, which is also quite wary. It is generally seen flying high over the forested mountain slopes, heading either to its next food source or to its roost site in the evening, and it has an extensive repertoire of calls.

Festive Amazon *Amazona festiva* 33cm

Vaughan Ashby

Locally distributed along the rivers of north-eastern Ecuador, this species of parrot tends to favour riverside forest habitats, such as areas close to oxbow lakes and seasonally flooded forest (Várzea). It is most regularly encountered along the Rio Napo and Rio Aguarico, and less commonly on the Rio Pastaza. Unlike the next species, this bird does not display a bright orange or red 'speculum' (block of coloured feathers on the inner wing). It is a rather uniform green, but does show a red band across its forehead and a red rump and lower back in flight although, of course, this cannot be seen when the bird is viewed from below. It has a distinctive '*rroww, rroww, rroww*' call.

Orange-winged Amazon *Amazona amazonica* 31-33cm

Vaughan Ashby

This is generally a quite common parrot of the eastern lowland forests of Ecuador and is locally numerous, particularly in Várzea and riverside forest. Its most obvious feature, whether at rest or in flight, is its very striking yellow face. In flight the bright orange 'speculum' on the inner wing is a good clue to its identity. It is often seen from boats, flying across rivers, commuting between feeding areas in the morning or going to roost in the evening, generally on wooded river islands. Typically in the fashion of the parrots of the genus *Amazona*, when it flies it employs very shallow wing beats. It has many calls, but in flight it usually utters a relatively high-pitched '*kewik, kewik, kewik*' or '*kwik, kwik, kwik*' sound.

Blue-and-yellow Macaw *Ara ararauna* 83cm

This is one of the largest and most instantly recognizable of the parrots, with beautiful blue and yellow plumage and a long tail. Still common in areas of intact lowland forest east of the Andes, these spectacular birds are most often seen crossing rivers in pairs or threes as they commute from one place to another. One of the three will be a youngster. Like most birds of the parrot family, this species routinely attends the gatherings at clay licks on riverbanks, where it digs out and swallows the mineral-rich earth. This is assumed to help in the digestion of certain fruits, but the gatherings are clearly also social events, with the birds spending much time interacting with each other.

Red-and-green Macaw *Ara chloroptera* 96cm

Another large and beautiful member of the parrot family, this bird is similar to the Scarlet Macaw *A. macao*, but is darker red and lacks yellow wing patches. It also displays prominent facial striping, actually lines of tiny red feathers. Like other macaws, it has a loud and raucous call. It can be seen in congregations of some numbers at several specific places in the eastern lowlands of Ecuador, where the birds gather to socialize and eat minerals.

Scarlet Macaw *Ara macao* 84-91cm

Vaughan Ashby

This close relative of the Red-and-green Macaw, *A. chloroptera*, is still quite common in the remote forested areas of the eastern lowlands of Ecuador, especially in areas of terra firma forest. It differs from that species by the lack of the lines of feathers on the face. It also has yellow bands on the upper wing and is a brighter red. However, this is not always apparent when viewing the bird and depends on the light conditions. Like other large macaws, members of this species are usually seen in pairs or groups of three or four birds, which almost certainly constitute family groups. They can, however, form larger groups when gathering to take mineral clay. Their loud, raucous calls are difficult to distinguish from those of the other macaws.

Squirrel Cuckoo *Piaya cayana* 40cm

This species is the most common member of the *Piaya* genus of cuckoos. It is often seen in the lowland forests of eastern Ecuador and also on the western Andean slope in the north, where there is forest. It is a large and obvious bird, with a long tail with white tips, bright rufous plumage, a conspicuous yellow bill, and a bright red orbital ring around the eye, and is hard to miss as it crashes around in the trees, hunting for caterpillars and other prey. Its call might be transcribed as '*Kick yooooooou*', the first note having an upwards inflection, the second note a downwards one.

Little Cuckoo *Piaya minuta* 27cm

As its name suggests, this is one of the smallest members of the *Piaya* cuckoos, and it is typical of the genus in having a rich rufous plumage. It has a much shorter tail than its cousin, the Squirrel Cuckoo, *P. cyana*, but shares the white tail-tips of its larger relative. It is an inhabitant of Ecuador's eastern humid lowlands and is found in quite marginal habitats, such as forest edge and dense secondary growth, often close to water. It is more often heard than seen, and is a much less common species in Ecuador than its larger and longer-tailed relative, despite not being a forest inhabitant.

Greater Ani *Crotophaga major* 48cm

This is typically a bird of the thick riverbank foliage along the streams and rivers of the eastern lowland forests of Ecuador. At first glance it appears to be a large and ungainly black bird with a long tail, but in bright conditions it can be seen to be beautifully iridescent, showing blue and green reflections off its upperparts and purple and violet reflections off its tail. It is generally seen moving in groups through dense riverside vegetation or flying across steams and rivers. The Greater Ani is a much larger bird than the Smooth-billed Ani, *C. ani*, which is a considerably dowdier relative and a bird that can be seen on the Galapagos Islands, where it has been introduced.

Hoatzin *Opisthocomus hoazin* 63cm

birdholidays.co.uk

The Hoatzin is one of the most unusual birds in the world, for a variety of reasons. Firstly, it would be hard to design such an odd-looking creature. Secondly, its habits and unique adaptations, including being a ruminant, set it apart from all other birds. Its flamboyant headdress, the complex patterns on its wings, a long, pale-tipped tail and its strange calls make it one of the most immediately recognizable forest birds of the Amazon region. The young birds have hooks on their wings, which enable them to move around in trees in a reptilian style, and the birds also possess the ability to dive underwater to escape predators. Due to their diet of semi-toxic leaves they tend to exude an unpleasant smell.

Tropical Screech Owl *Megascops choliba* 22cm

birdholidays.co.uk

This is just one of no less than eight species of screech owl in the *Megascops* genus that occur in Ecuador, and just one genus of a family represented by an amazing total of twenty-eight species. There is probably no other country on Earth of a similar size where there are so many different owls. This one is the most common and most widespread of the screech owls, and therefore the one most likely to be seen. It occurs in many habitats, including parks and gardens in towns. Its call is commonly heard at night, an accelerating series of notes that ascends the scale then abruptly stops, usually but not always with a couple of accentuated notes at the end – perhaps '*ou ou ou ou ou ou ou OOK OOK*'.

Rufescent Screech Owl *Megascops ingens* 25–28cm

This typically cryptic and beautifully plumaged screech owl is another member of the *Megascops* genus found in Ecuador. The taxonomic status of the group is still in a state of flux as ornithologists try to work out the actual identity of each known type. Many of the screech owls are birds of the Andean slopes, which are difficult to access, especially during the night when these birds are active. The key to unravelling the problem is sophisticated analysis of the birds' vocalizations. Although rather poorly known, it would appear that this particular species is widely distributed on both sides of the Andes at subtropical to temperate elevations.

Ferruginous Pygmy Owl *Glaucidium brasilianum* 16.5cm

The most common member of the six species of pygmy owl in Ecuador, this bird occurs in the humid eastern lowlands and the lower foothills on the eastern side of the Andes. Its plumage is very variable, but it usually has a rufous tone to its general appearance. The crown is generally finely streaked but it can appear almost plain. The bird's call is a low, short, hollow whistle repeated at about three notes to a second, '*hu…hu…hu…hu …hu…hu…hu…hu… hu…*', and it is easily imitated. This species is replaced at higher elevations along the Andean slope by the Andean Pygmy Owl, *G. jardinii*, and the Subtropical Pygmy Owl, *G. parkeri*. The other three Ecuadorian pygmy owl species occur on the Pacific slope and the western lowlands.

'San Isidro' Owl *Strix* sp. (as yet not named) About 50cm

This bird was discovered recently by ornithologist Mitch Lysinger on his property, Cabanas San Isidro, at an elevation of about 2,000m on the eastern Andean slope. It closely resembles the Black-banded Owl, *Ciccaba huhula*, which occurs at much lower elevations and sounds very similar. However, it is a considerably larger bird. A common trait among closely related species is that those at lower elevations are generally smaller than their close relatives that occur at higher elevations. This species can presently (2008) be seen hunting moths at the lights just outside the lodge at San Isidro. A mysterious and enigmatic bird, it is hopefully to be found elsewhere at similar elevations in other localities, where its forest habitat remains and a road provides access.

Eustace Barnes

Short-eared Owl *Asio flammeus* 34-42cm

Vaughan Ashby

Incredible as it may seem, there are two species of owl on the Galapagos Islands and both are represented by endemic subspecies. This species (subspecies *A. f. galapagoensis*) is thought to have a population of about 9,000 birds, spread across almost the entire archipelago. This means that the birds are rather thinly spread, making this a somewhat uncommon resident. The other owl resident on the islands is the Barn Owl, *Tyto alba*, of the endemic race *T. a. punctatissima*, which has a population roughly similar in numbers to that of the Short-eared Owl. Interestingly, both species are also found in continental Ecuador – this species in high Páramo and the Barn Owl mostly in the western lowlands. They are quite clearly both successful and adaptive species.

65

Rufous Potoo *Nyctibius bracteatus* 25-26cm

This beautiful creature is a mysterious denizen of the lowland tropical forests of the Amazon basin. It is by far the smallest of the potoos, of which there are five species in Ecuador. Its lovely russet plumage with bold white spots is unique. It is very rarely seen unless it takes up residence close to one of the 'jungle' lodges, where it might be heard and then hopefully located at its daytime roosting place. A bird tends to use the same roost perch for some considerable time. The species' call is a

moderately descending series of short notes, '*Who-o-o-o-o-o-o-o-o-o-o-o-o*' (*The Birds of Ecuador*, Ridgely and Greenfield).

Common Potoo *Nyctibius griseus* 38cm

This species is generally found in lowland forested areas, although it does seem to prefer more open habitats than some of its larger relatives, such as the Great Potoo, *N. grandis*, and the Long-tailed Potoo, *N. aethereus*. In most places this is the most common of the six species of this cryptic, nocturnal group of birds found in Ecuador. All of these species are strictly insectivorous and spend the day in a motionless position, disguised as part of the tree in which they are perched. This species has a beautiful mournful call, which consists of 4–5 descending notes. It is a strange and unmistakable call that can be heard as dusk descends in the locations where this mysterious bird occurs.

Lesser Nighthawk *Chordeiles acutipennis* 20cm

Vaughan Ashby

Members of the nightjar family, the nighthawks are characterized by their long, pointed wings, which give them a somewhat falcon-like shape. When combined with their fast and aerobatic flight, this sets them apart from most of the numerous nightjar species in Ecuador. Seven of these species are nighthawks, and this one is the smallest. It closely resembles the Common Nighthawk, *C. minor*, a migrant to Ecuador that has been recorded occasionally on the Galapagos Islands. This species occurs in open areas, where it can be seen hawking for insects at dawn and dusk.

Pauraque *Nytidromus albicollis* 26-28cm

One of the most widespread members of the nightjar family in low-land Ecuador, on both sides of the Andes, usually at below 1,200m, the Pauraque commonly occurs in marginal habitats, including cleared areas close to human habitation and secondary growth. It is not generally found inside primary forest, but often sits on tracks and roads running through forested areas, where it is most often and most easily seen. The first indication of its presence is nearly always its unique and somewhat ethereal wailing call, which rises and falls and is a very distinctive and familiar sound. The species has a lovely plumage pattern of very bold markings on the upperparts, and the male flashes white in the tail.

Blackish Nightjar *Caprimulgus nigrescens* 20cm

This nightjar is a bird of the terra firma forests of Ecuador's eastern lowlands, where it is typically found roosting around rocky outcrops, sometimes on bare rock. Although it is a very dark nightjar (hence its name), it can appear much paler in bright sunlight. The photograph shows a female in such a situation, sitting out on bare rock in the blistering midday heat, where she was beautifully camouflaged and was not seen until she flew as the author nearly stepped on her. Typically, this bird did not move very far and soon settled again, relying on her cryptic plumage to conceal her. The male shows white corners to the tail.

Lyre-tailed Nightjar *Uropsalis lyra*
Male 75–80cm; Female 21–23cm

The most obvious feature of this beautiful nightjar is the male's extraordinarily long, double-pronged tail, which is reflected in the difference in the measurements for male and female. It occurs at middle elevations in forest on both slopes of the Andes. Male birds fly over fast-flowing mountain streams at dusk, displaying their fabulous tails. The female (depicted) is a much more anonymous creature, lacking the male's wonderful tail adornments. Both sexes have a dark, cryptic plumage and a rusty collar around the back of the neck. The birds occur at 800–2,500m, and regularly utilize the rocky sides of man-made road cuts for nesting and roosting.

68

White-collared Swift *Streptoprocne zonaris* 21cm

Of an incredible total of 15 swift species that occur in Ecuador, this is the largest. It is likely to be seen in almost any part of the country, as it wanders widely – it can be found on either side of the Andes, in the tropical lowlands and along the Andean mountain flanks, sometimes even as high as 4,000m elevation. The adult sports a contrasting white collar, but depending on age, the young birds do not necessarily display this feature. Encountering a roving flock of these common but spectacular swifts can be a very exciting, if sometimes short-lived, experience. The sound of the air whooshing through their wings as they pass at high speed is remarkable.

Short-tailed Swift *Chaetura brachyura* 11cm

Vaughan Ashby

This is a common small swift of the eastern Amazonian lowlands and possibly the one most often seen, usually flying very fast and erratically over the forest. It is one of the 15 swift species in Ecuador, of which 6 belong to the genus *Chaetura* – a genus that contains many similar species, which are notoriously difficult to identify. The bird's tail is very short, giving it a unique profile and making it the most distinctive and easiest of these species to identify. For a swift, it has an extremely rapid, bat-like flight and rather short, paddle-shaped wings. Its pale caramel-coloured rump and upper tail are distinctive. It is a very different member of the family from the previous species.

Sword-billed Hummingbird *Ensifera ensifera* 13cm

One of the most extraordinary birds in the world, this hummingbird has a bill as long as or even longer than its body, so although the bird's length is supposedly about 13cm, much of this is the bill. This amazing adaptation enables it to feed from long, trumpet-shaped flowers of plants such as daturas. It is found on the east Andean slope at typical elevations of about 2,000–3,000m, where there are abundant shrubs with these typically tube-like hanging flowers. It is, of course, instantly recognizable, although it is an uncommon bird. It is seen with some regularity along the road from Quito to Tena at about 2,500–3,000m elevation on the east side of the Papallacta Pass, for instance in the gardens in Papallacta village and at the feeders at Guango Lodge.

Tyrian Metaltail *Metallura tyrianthina* 10cm

Of the four species of metaltail in Ecuador, this is by far the most common and widespread. It is one of the most common hummingbirds in the highlands of Ecuador at about 2,100–3,800m elevation. It inhabits cloud forest and in particular forest-edge habitats, as well as more open, scrubby areas, wherever there are flowering trees and shrubs. The male has a rich copper-coloured tail and is generally only moderately iridescent, but has a brighter glittering throat. The female (depicted) is a pale buffish colour below with a white spot behind the eye. The bird's bill is short and straight.

birdholidays.co.uk

Glittering-throated Emerald *Amazilia fimbriata* 8.5cm

Generally common throughout its range, as it does not appear to have any specific habitat preference, this hummingbird seems to be found in any place where there is flowering shrubbery, apart from forests, which it shuns. Birds of this species regularly come to feeders but they are not dominant, since they are quite small and do not gather in large groups to defend feeders. The birds usually occur singly or as a pair. This species generally appears as rather dull dark green with only moderate iridescence, but the male flashes a bright, glittering, emerald-coloured throat at certain angles. Perhaps the best feature for purposes of identification is the bird's white belly, which extends up the centre of the breast in both sexes.

Purple-bibbed Whitetip *Urosticte benjamini*
Male 9cm; Female 7.5cm

This is a scarce bird of the lower foothills of the west slope, found at an elevation of up to about 1,600m. It occurs principally in the lower levels and borders of humid forest. The male (depicted) is a handsome little bird and well named, with his shining purple 'bib'. He also has a somewhat curious tail pattern, with the two central tail feathers tipped with white. The female, as usual, is far more discreet in her attire, but her outer tail feathers are tipped with  white. Although glittering green above she lacks the purple bib, and her underparts are white densely spotted with shining green.

Booted Racquet-tail *Ocreatus underwoodii*
Male 11.5; Female 7cm.

Eustace Barnes

Although uncommon, this species is generally found on both Andean slopes at about 900–2,200m, but is more numerous in the west. Splendidly reflected in the bird's very apt name, the most obvious features of the male are its 'boots' and the 'racquets' on the tips of its elongated tail feathers. The boots are very similar to those worn by the pufflegs of the genus *Eriocnemis*, but the pufflegs do not sport the fantastic tail of this species. Neither does the female Booted Racquet-tail, which closely resembles the female of the Purple-bibbed Whitetip, *Urosticte benjamini*, but shows less shining green below. The males from the east slope sport rich buff boots. The photo depicts a bird from the west slope.

Empress Brilliant *Heliodoxa imperatrix*
Male 14cm; Female 12.2cm

Eustace Barnes

This scarce hummingbird is large and subtly beautiful. It is probably most easily seen at feeders along the lower part of Ecuador's Tandayapa Valley, not far from Quito and close to the famous 'birding resort' of Mindo, on the west Andean slope. Although not sporting particularly bright colours, the male is generally glittering green, brighter on the belly with an inconspicuous violet-purple patch on the lower throat. He is perhaps best characterized by his relatively long and deeply forked tail. The female bird is heavily spotted below.

72

Fawn-breasted Brilliant *Heliodoxa rubinoides*

Male 11cm; Female 10cm

Found on both the east and west slopes of the Andes, in subtropical forest at 1,100–2,100m, this close relative of the preceding species is not rare but also not particularly common. It readily comes to feeders. It is the only highland hummer that displays a combination of deep glittering green and buff underparts. Birds on the west slope display more coppery-bronze reflections on their uppersides than do east-slope birds. Both sexes have a lovely glittering pink throat-patch, although this is smaller in females than in males.

Eustace Barnes

Long-tailed Sylph *Aglaiocercus kingi* 10cm (not including tail)

Eustace Barnes

Mainly a bird of the east slope of the Andes, this species can also be found on the west slope in the north of Ecuador. As its name indicates, the male sports a magnificent iridescent, forked tail, which can be up to 9cm long. This can appear blue-green to turquoise in colour, depending on the angle of refraction. The male also has a glittering violet-blue throat-patch. The female is green above and bright buff below. A sibling species, the Violet-tailed Sylph, *A. coelestis*, is very similar, but flashes turquoise to violet-blue colours on the tail and is found on the western slope. The female of this species sports a glittering blue crown as opposed to the green of the female Long-tailed Sylph.

73

Long-billed Starthroat *Heliomaster longirostris* 9.5cm

This hummingbird occurs in forest edge and clearings in Ecuador's lowlands, up to about 1,200m elevation, but usually below 700m. It is most commonly seen on the western side of the Andes. It is characterized by its very long, almost straight bill, which makes it adept at reaching into long, trumpet-shaped flowers. It also flycatches small insects, often over water. The bird depicted is either a female or an immature individual. The male has an irridescent blue crown, although both sexes always have the broad white 'moustache' on the sides of the dark throat (an irridescent pinkish-purple in the male).

Gorgeted Woodstar *Chaetocercus heliodor*
Male 8.7cm; Female 7.1cm

Female   Male

This tiny hummingbird is very scarce, but it can be found in the forest canopy and edge along both Andean slopes at 1,100–1,800m. It is not generally a garden bird but can be seen visiting the feeders at Guango Lodge, on the road to Tena. It is bee-like in flight, generally moving quite slowly, but with extremely fast wing beats. (It is a general rule that the smaller the hummingbird, the faster are its wing beats.) The male of this species is characterized by his very dark colour, his gorget, which is elongated at the sides, and his dusky belly. The female has a buff throat that becomes rufous on the belly.

74

Velvet-purple Coronet *Boissonneaua jardini* 12.7cm

This bird is arguably the most beautiful of Ecuador's incredible total of 132 hummingbird species. It is a bird of the west Andean slope, in the north of the country. Rather uncommon, it seasonally visits feeders in such places as the Mindo Lindo guesthouse, situated on the main highway above Mindo town. Its natural environment is the canopy and borders of the foothill forest, at about 800–1,700m elevation, but it probably makes altitudinal migrations or movements depending on particular food sources.

Eustace Barnes

Buff-winged Starfrontlet *Coeligena lutetiae* 14.5cm

Eustace Barnes

This is quite a common hummingbird of the higher cloud forest along the eastern Andean slope and the western slope in the north. It is unmistakable as both sexes are the only hummers to have the distinctive buff wing-patch, offset by the deep blackish tone of the upperparts. The male is glittering green below. The female is densely mottled-green below, with a cinnamon-buff throat. In typical starfrontlet fashion, it does indeed have a shining frontlet and a very long, straight bill. It is a fast-flying species that might be seen zooming over a forest or down a valley, perhaps heading for the next lodge with some feeders.

Black-throated Mango
Anthracothorax nigricollis 12.4–14cm

birdholidays.co.uk

This hummingbird often chooses to nest in the most exposed places. The bird depicted is a female, which is distinguished by the black stripe that runs down from her throat to her belly and is graphically offset by the otherwise white underparts. The male has a solid black throat and breast, and he can look completely dark in poor light. This is a relatively large hummingbird of semi-open areas, woodland borders and secondary growth in the lowlands on both sides of the Andes, often near water. It is regularly seen catching insects rather than feeding at flowers, and is generally quite common.

Blue-crowned Trogon *Trogon curucui* 25cm

birdholidays.co.uk

Found in the eastern lowlands of Ecuador at up to about 1,100m, this trogon does not necessarily require a true forest habitat and is the species commonly seen along the relatively open forest borders. Both sexes are characterized by the whitish band separating the dark breast from the red belly. In the male the breast is deep iridescent blue becoming deep green on the mantle. The female (depicted) has a grey breast and a pinkish-red belly, separated by a much broader and more diffuse white band. The undertail in both the male and female is always barred. Like other trogon species, this one is susceptible to imitations of its call and often comes to investigate even a moderately accurate impersonation.

Masked Trogon *Trogon personatus* 26cm

The only truly highland trogon, this species occurs in the cloud forests of the eastern Andean slope from about 700m almost up to the tree line. The very similar Collared Trogon, *T. collaris*, occurs at lower elevations. The Masked Trogon is similarly patterned to some other members of the genus, with a sharply demarcated white band across the breast. The male with his striking plumage is unmistakable, and the bird's hooting call is unique and distinctive in the higher levels of its range. The females of both species are different from the males, having rich brown upperparts, but the female Masked Trogon has a blacker face and throat than the female Collared Trogon.

Amazonian White-tailed Trogon *Trogon viridis* 30cm

This is a common inhabitant of the forests of the eastern lowlands of Ecuador. As is usual, the female has a far more subdued plumage than the splendid male, who sports a dazzling deep blue head and upper body plumage. This is replaced by grey in the female, but both sexes have clear yellow underparts. The bird is very often heard rather than seen and its call is a distinctive series of identical notes with a yelping quality repeated over and over, '*kyow…kyow… kyow…kyow…kyow…*', and so on. As is usual in trogons, it readily comes to investigate an imitation call, thus providing excellent views. Also like all other trogon species, this one hunts by sitting quietly, peering around for prey before flitting to a new perch.

Male (main) and female (left)

Pavonine Quetzal *Pharomachrus pavoninus* 33–34cm

This bird of the lowland forests of eastern Ecuador is scarce and generally highly dispersed. Its double-noted call is confusing because it can sound as though it has been given from a distant perch when it may be much closer; at other times, it may in fact be a long way off. As a member of the trogon family, it is typical in being very territorial, often flying in from some distance to perch overhead in response to tape playback – but note that this luring method is a huge annoyance to birds like trogons and quetzals, and if done regularly may cause them to desert a territory (see also page 9).

Golden-headed Quetzal
Pharomachrus auriceps 33.5–35.5cm

Vaughan Ashby

This denizen of the cloud forests of both the eastern and western Andean slopes is a fabulous creature. It is usually fairly common and occurs at about 1,000–2,800m. Its resonant call is the key to locating it, as it is easily mimicked and the bird will respond with gusto, often flying in to investigate the perceived threat from a rival. It can sometimes be seen or heard in the same areas as its close relative, the Crested Quetzal, *P. antisianus*, but this species tends to be more numerous at higher elevations. The bright emerald upperparts of the Golden-headed Quetzal contrast with the more golden hue of the bird's head.

Ringed Kingfisher *Megaceryle torquata* 40cm

The largest of all the neotropical kingfishers, this bird is common along lowland rivers and other wetlands on both sides of the Andes. It is very easily identified by its large size, colouration and very large bill. Both sexes have grey upperparts, but the male (depicted) has a completely reddish belly; although the female has similar rufous underparts, she has a grey band across the breast separated from the belly by a narrow white band. The bird also has a loud, rattling call that usually indicates its presence in advance. Despite being relatively common, it is a spectacular member of the riverside bird community. Its close relative the Belted Kingfisher, *M. alcyon*, is an uncommon visitor to the Galapagos Islands.

Amazon Kingfisher *Chloroceryle amazona* 30cm

By far the largest of the three Amazonian green kingfishers, this bird has a massive, dagger-like bill. Both sexes have beautiful deep green upperparts and largely white underparts. The male has a chestnut-orange breast band, while the female has largely white underparts. The species has a fast and powerful flight, although this is not as speedy as the flight of its smaller relative, the Green Kingfisher, *C. americana*. It differs from the smaller Green-and-rufous Kingfisher, *C. inda*, with its white rather than rufous underparts. The Amazon Kingfisher is a common bird of the rivers of Ecuador's eastern lowlands, and is therefore one of the birds commonly seen from boats.

79

Green Kingfisher *Chloroceryle americana* 20cm

Rather similar to the larger Amazon Kingfisher, *C. amazona*, and also quite common but less conspicuous, partly due to its smaller size, this species tends to live along smaller streams than its larger congener. It is often seen flashing past in very rapid flight, and when viewed at close range its beautiful deep green, iridescent plumage becomes apparent. Like in the previous species, the male is more colourful than the female, with a bright reddish-chestnut breast band, while the female is white and pale cream below with a green breast band. This species also has a shorter crest than its larger cousin, the Amazon Kingfisher. Relative to its size, it possibly has the largest bill of any of the neotropical kingfishers.

Pygmy Kingfisher *Chloroceryle aenea* 13.5cm

The smallest of the American kingfishers and perhaps the most attractive, this bird can be remarkably tame when encountered in a small boat. It often sits quietly by the side of the smallest of streams, frequently under overhanging vegetation, which makes it very difficult to spot despite its brilliant multicoloured plumage. It is also sometimes difficult to see in flight, on account of its small size and very rapid flight. Its deep green head and upperparts, separated by an orange and cream-coloured collar and deep reddish chestnut underparts, make for a striking pattern. The bird feeds on tiny fish, as expected from a kingfisher of its size.

Green-and-rufous Kingfisher *Chloroceryle inda* 22cm

Phil Palmer

This species is much less common than either the Amazon King-fisher, *C. amazona*, or its smaller relative the Green Kingfisher, *C. americana*. It is a beautiful bird that is most often seen along slow-flowing forest streams like quiet backwaters of Ecuador where, like the Pygmy Kingfisher, *C. aenea*, it can be very tame when approached in a small boat. It hunts in a similar fashion to that species, but is less conspicuous and prefers low and often some-what obscured vantage points. It will definitely not be seen hunt-ing from roadside telegraph wires with its larger and bolder rela-tives. It can also be found, on rare occurrences, in the lowlands of north-western Ecuador.

Blue-crowned Motmot *Momotus momota* 41cm

This member of a fabulously attractive family is probably the most common motmot of the region, and is found in a variety of wooded habitats, including secondary forest. The beautiful electric-blue stripes on the head and the black mask are the most obvi-ous features of this lovely bird. It has warm chestnut-hued underparts, contrasting with vivid deep green upperparts. Its tail is characterized by bare quills with spatula-shaped tips. These are actually made by the bird itself, by plucking out the feather barbs to leave a bare shaft. This behaviour is common to some other mem-bers of the family, as is its habit of sitting quietly and waiting for prey to show.

Broad-billed Motmot *Electron platyrhynchum* 35 cm

This is an unusual motmot in having a very different call from the typical '*mo mo*' that gives the motmots their name. Its call is a rather strange, growling noise that sounds a bit like a cicada, or even a short burst from a distant chainsaw. Its orange-rufous breast with a black spot in the centre is distinctive, but not entirely diagnostic, as it resembles that of the Rufous Motmot, *Baryphthengus martii*. That species also has a thicker and less down-curved bill, more extensive rufous on the underparts and a smaller black breast spot; it is also a considerably larger bird.

White-necked Puffbird
Notharchus macrorhynchos 25cm

Ron Hoff

Large and strikingly patterned, this puffbird is a spectacular creature that – like many other members of the family – is a 'wait-and-see' hunter. It sits quietly in the mid-canopy waiting to ambush prey, and is capable of tackling many larger prey items than those pursued by other puffbirds, including large insects, lizards, frogs and even small snakes. It has a white throat and forehead, a thick black band across the breast, finely barred flanks and black upperparts. Although this species is widely distributed in both the western and eastern lowland forests of Ecuador, it is an uncommon bird throughout most parts of its range.

Pied Puffbird *Notharchus tectus* 14.5–17cm

This small black and white-coloured puffbird is found in the humid forested lowlands on both sides of the Andes. It is a bird of the subcanopy and borders, where it usually sits quietly and can be remarkably inconspicuous. Although it is sometimes more conspicuous when it is perched in open areas, it is often only noticed when it sallies after prey. It frequently sits in close proximity to its mate. Birds from the east of the Andes (depicted) are somewhat larger, with a broader breast-band and rather more white spotting on the fore-crown. This

Phil Palmer

species could only realistically be confused with the White-necked Puffbird, *N. macrorhynchos*, but that bird is much larger. The Pied Puffbird's shrill, piping song is also distinctive once recognized.

Black-streaked Puffbird
Malacoptila fulvogularis 19–23 cm

This lovely though relatively subtly plumaged puffbird is unusual in that it occurs at higher altitudes than most of its relatives. It is found in lower temperate and upper tropical-level cloud forest at elevations of approximately 1,100–2,100m, on the east Andean slope. Although resembling several other puffbird species, it does not overlap with them in its altitudinal range. Its orange-buff throat with white moustachial marks is diagnostic. It has a dark, streaked head, brown upperparts and a boldly streaked belly. An uncommon bird, it may in fact be seen less often than it might be because it sits still for long periods and does not attract attention.

Ron Hoff

83

White-fronted Nunbird *Monasa morphoeus* 27-28 cm

Although sharing the coral-red bill of the widespread and common Black-fronted Nunbird, *M. nigrifrons*, this member of the nunbird family is the only one to display the contrasting white 'face' that so characterizes the species. Because it is a bird of terra firma forest it does not overlap with its close relative, which inhabits the swampy Várzea forest along the lowland river systems. It frequents the middle and upper storeys of its forest habitat, and ranges up into the lower foothills along the base of the Andes. Like its close relative it often bursts into 'song', which tends to be given as a rollicking and garbled duet, or even joined by several birds as if infectious.

Swallow-winged Puffbird *Chelidoptera tenebrosa* 16 cm

This is a somewhat aberrant member of the puffbird clan that displays different behaviour from that of all the other members of the family. Its modus operandi is to sally out from high perches to capture flying insect prey. In this respect its behaviour more closely resembles that of a large flycatcher such as a kingbird or a kiskadee. It has a very short tail and very broad, blunt wings, which it uses to glide back to its vantage point after a foray. Deep blue-black above with a whitish vent, it may appear uniformly black when silhouetted against the sky. It is particularly fond of hawking over water, and is therefore often seen from boats plying the waterways of the eastern lowlands of Ecuador.

White-throated Toucan *Ramphastos tucanus* 54-57cm

A very character-istic bird of the eastern forested lowland, this toucan is quite common in suitable forest habitat and is not hunted or trapped. Sadly, Ecuador's toucans are too often seen caged in markets, though this species' calls are still one of the most often heard sounds echoing through the forest. They consist of a far-carrying sound with a yelping quality – to the author's ears sounding much like puppies. Also known as Cuvier's Toucan, this species is almost identical in appearance to the Channel-billed Toucan, *R. vitellinus*, with which it occurs widely. However, that species has a very different call, which is a repeated growling croak.

Grey-breasted Mountain Toucan
Andigena hypoglauca 46cm

This beautiful toucan is one of three montane species that occur in Ecuador. Its distinctive yelping calls are easily imitated, and the bird will often come to investigate if this is done. It has a very attractive plumage pattern with a contrasting array of colours: a blue-grey body, blackish head, olive-green upperparts and a bright yellow rump. It also has an amazingly ornate bill, with a combination of black, yellow and red. It can be seen at about 2,500–3,300m elevation, along roads that traverse the east Andean slope.

Chestnut-eared Aracari *Pteroglossus castanotis* 43cm

The aracaris, although clearly members of the toucan family, are very different from the larger, mostly black and white *Ramphastos* species, having contrasting yellow- and red-banded underparts, and mostly blackish upperparts. They are also typified by having a long tail that is particularly conspicuous in flight. This is rather laboured, making the birds look as though they are having to work hard to stay in the air. They are often seen crossing rivers in small, loose flocks, usually one at a time. Six species in the *Pteroglossus* genus occur in Ecuador – this is usually the most common and the one most often seen by visitors to the lowland forests of the east.

Red-necked Woodpecker *Campephilus rubricollis* 34cm

Ron Hoff

This large and boldly marked woodpecker is a scarce inhabitant of the lowland Amazonian rainforests of eastern Ecuador. It has a crested red head and neck, and chestnut underparts. The male bird has a small black and white spot on the ear coverts, and the female has a white stripe from the base of the bill. This woodpecker's presence is frequently indicated by the distinctive sound of its 'drum', which typically is made by banging very loudly and rapidly twice on a tree, and could be transcribed as '*ba bang*'. This sound can be heard more than a kilometre away in still conditions. The bird's call is a loud, rasping '*kyaah*'.

Crimson-crested Woodpecker
Campephilus melanoleucus 31cm

Although not a member of the same genus as the Lineated Woodpecker, *Dryocopus lineatus*, this species is more than superficially similar. It shares the high, pointed red crest and the same general pattern of plumage, with white stripes on the neck and back, and barred underparts. However, with a good view, you may be able to see that, unlike in the Lineated Woodpecker, the white scapular stripes on the upperparts of this species meet in the centre of the back. The bird has a powerful, resonant 'double-knock' drum, whereas the Lineated Woodpecker generally performs a slow 'drum roll' and has a loud '*wicka wicka wicka*' call. It is replaced west of the Andes by the Guayaquil Woodpecker, *C. guayaquilensis*.

Vaughan Ashby

Yellow-throated Woodpecker *Piculus flavigula* 19-20cm

This woodpecker is a bird of the eastern lowland forest of Ecuador and is most often encountered in terra firma forest, where it clambers up and around the larger limbs of the trees. It can be seen at all levels in the forest, sometimes moving with mixed species flocks and very often as a pair, foraging separately. Both sexes display the characteristic yellow throat, although the female lacks the bright red crown of the male. An attractive member of the woodpecker family, this species occasionally utters a shrill, hissing and high-pitched '*shweeeeer*' call.

Golden-green Woodpecker
Piculus chrysochloros 18-24cm

Phil Palmer

Another of the six species of *Piculus* woodpecker that occur in Ecuador, this bird is a scarce and local member of the clan found only in the lowland forests of the east. Two other species of *Piculus* occur in the same range and habitat, the previous species and the White-throated Woodpecker, *P. leucolaemus*. However, both are rather different and never display the evenly banded underparts shown by the female bird in the picture. Female woodpeckers tend to display little of the male's red headdress, and in this species they show none.

Yellow-tufted Woodpecker
Melanerpes cruentatus 20cm

Vaughan Ashby

As is usual of birds in the *Melanerpes* genus, this beautiful species roams around in small but noisy flocks and is usually heard first, since it makes a very distinctive, high-pitched, 'twittering' call, such as '*krr, krr, krr…*'. It also has the usual rather clown-like plumage so typical of this group of woodpeckers, being mostly blue-black with a red crown, a yellow eye-ring and a stripe running back from the eye. The rump is contrastingly white and the belly red, with fine black and white barring on the flanks. The Yellow-tufted Woodpecker is an inhabitant of the lowland rainforests of eastern Ecuador and is common in suitable habitats, where it is regularly encountered.

Gilded Barbet *Capito auratus* 20cm

Vaughan Ashby

A member of the family Capitidonae, which is closely related to the toucans, this was formerly considered a subspecies of the Black-spotted Barbet, *C. niger*, and as is usual with the *Capito* barbets, it is a very handsome creature indeed. It is a bird of tropical moist lowland forest of the east, especially terra firma forest. It mainly occurs in Ecuador's eastern lowlands, but also ranges into the lower foothills of the eastern Andean slope. It is largely frugivorous. Like other barbets, the Gilded Barbet is a thickset, fairly large-headed bird, with a stubby bill. In females, the throat is streaked black. Both sexes have dark maroon irides, greyish legs and a broadly black-tipped grey bill.

Plain-brown Woodcreeper *Dendrocincla fuliginosa* 20cm

Vaughan Ashby

This uniformly plumaged woodcreeper is common in the forests of the lowlands and lower Andean foothills on both sides of the Andes. As its name suggests, it is a bird with little in the way of distinguishing markings in its plumage. It has the typical rufescent wings and tail of a woodcreeper, and is slightly paler and rather warmer hued on the underparts. It displays a relatively subtle face pattern, having somewhat greyer ear coverts and a darker but not particularly significant malar stripe. It may attend swarms of army ants, but is not as closely tied to this habit as its close relative, the White-chinned Woodcreeper, *D. merula*, which is very similar but has pale blue eyes and, of course, a white chin.

Cinnamon-throated Woodcreeper
Dendrexetastes rufigula 25cm

Vaughan Ashby

An uncommon resident of the forested eastern lowlands of Ecuador, this is more a bird of the forest edge than of the interior. It is a big, uniformly rusty-coloured member of the family, characterized by the variable pattern of crisply bordered, droplet-shaped white spots on the breast. It has a straight and heavy pale green bill. It is often heard just before dawn, and its ringing, ascending and descending calls are a great substitute for a birder's alarm clock where it occurs. This is especially true if there is a palm tree nearby, as this species is particularly partial to roosting in palms. It is rarely heard during the day.

Wedge-billed Woodcreeper
Glyphorynchus spirurus 14.5cm

Found in the lowland forest on both sides of the Andes, this tiny bird is generally one of the most common members of the woodcreeper clan. However, because of its small size, it can be unobtrusive and is thus sometimes overlooked, unless it is seen flying between trees. It is characterized by its uniform plumage, and in particular its short, chisel-shaped bill, which is unique among the family. It could be confused with the Plain Xenops, *Xenops minutus*, which is even smaller and feeds along the smallest lateral branches. It frequently occurs in the same areas as the Olivaceous Woodcreeper, *Sittasomus griseicapillus*, which is of a similar size and sometimes accompanies the same mixed species flocks. The Olivaceous Woodcreeper is also found in both the east and west of Ecuador, but is much more common in the west.

Straight-billed Woodcreeper *Xiphorhynchus picus* 21cm

This woodcreeper is well named and easily identified as it does indeed have the straightest bill of any member of the family. The bill is also very pointed and strikingly white. The bird is extensively spotted and streaked whitish around the head and breast. It is common in the eastern lowlands of Ecuador, and is found in a variety of wooded habitats, ranging from Várzea forest and forest borders to secondary woodland. Often quite conspicuous and tame, this bird is easy to observe because it prefers to forage in the lower and middle levels. Its descending, trilling call is given at various times of the day, rather than at dawn and dusk like the calls of many members of the family.

Vaughan Ashby

Red-billed Scythebill
Campylorhamphus trochilirostris 23-24cm

This extraordinary and spectacular member of the woodcreeper family is generally an uncommon bird within its range on both sides of the Andes, but can be found in a variety of wooded habitats. It is rare in the east, but more common in the west, where it ranges up into the foothills. Its strange, elongated and extremely decurved bill is presumably an adaptation to allow the bird to probe areas that other birds cannot. It has distinctive loud and strident calls, which descend the scale and are somewhat antbird-like. At higher elevations you may be lucky and encounter the large and very rare Greater Scythebill, *C. pucherani*. The Brown-billed Scythebill, *C. pusillus*, is much more likely to be seen in the humid subtropics of both slopes.

Phil Palmer

91

Streaked Xenops *Xenops rutilans* 12cm

Vaughan Ashby

This is a fairly common bird found in lowland wooded habitats in western Ecuador at up to about 2,000m, and in the forested eastern Andean slope at about 800–2,000m. The xenops are tiny members of the family Furnariidae, but are far removed from the typical members of the family such as the horneros. The xenops are typified by their habit of creeping along the tiniest of branches and often hanging upside down. The other three members of this strange but endearing group of arboreal birds are principally dwellers of lowland forest.

Bar-winged Cinclodes *Cinclodes fuscus* 18cm ✓

Vaughan Ashby

This is the most common and most widespread member of the *Cinclodes* genus, members of the ovenbird family, the Furnariidae. It is regularly seen along the sides of roads in the highlands at about 3,200–4,300m. Although it occurs in a variety of open habitats at high elevations, it is especially fond of damp areas such as Páramo, marshes, streams, lake margins and roadside ditches. At first glance it appears to be a plain brown bird with whitish underparts, but it is characterized by its wing pattern – its prominent wing-bar is very obvious when seen in flight.

Stout-billed Cinclodes *Cinclodes excelsior* 20.5cm

This close relative of the Bar-winged Cinclodes, *C. fuscus*, is also a bird of the high Páramo grasslands and may occur at even higher elevations. Although less likely to be seen in roadside ditches, it does use its 'stout bill' to probe wet places. However, there is a better chance to see it in areas that have a modest amount of low scrub, or in stunted polylepis woodland. Unlike its relative, it occasionally perches in these trees. It can readily be seen at the pass at Papallacta, as you cross the eastern edge of the Andes before dropping down into the eastern lowlands.

Yellow-chinned Spinetail *Certhiaxis cinnamomeus* 14cm

Occurring in the tropical lowlands east of the Andes, this member of the family of furnarids is always seen close to water, and in waterside or floating vegetation along rivers or on oxbow lakes. As well as being a characteristic bird of its habitat, it is typified by its yellow upper throat, although this feature is generally difficult to discern. Otherwise it is very similar to the Red-and-white Spinetail, *C. mustelinus*, but that species lacks the yellow throat and has blacker lores and a reddish crown that is the same colour as the mantle. In this species the forecrown is grey. Although fairly common in its habitat, it can be unobtrusive in the thick waterside cover.

93

Pacific Hornero *Furnarius cinnamomeus* 19cm

Phil Palmer

This is the archetypal ovenbird, building a very recognizable mud nest that closely resembles an old-fashioned clay oven, as used by a baker (*hornero* in Spanish). The nests are very solid structures, and although they are not usually reused by the birds themselves, they are often utilized by other species. They are a very characteristic feature in this part of the world, being placed prominently on telegraph poles, fence posts or horizontal tree limbs. Horneros have loud, staccato calls, which are often uttered annoyingly early in the morning as a duet. They are likely to be seen strutting around in any open or semi-open habitat west of the Andes, up to an elevation of about 2,300m in the far south.

Great Antshrike *Taraba major* 20cm

This species has a penchant for dense under-storey foliage at the forest edge and other woodland habitats, including secondary growth. Usually the first indication of its presence, its song consists of an accelerating series of hooting notes characterized by a final snarling note. This is a large and strikingly plumaged member of the antbird family. Both the male and the female are graphically bicoloured. Although both share the

burning red eyes, bright white underparts and expressive crest, the male is quite different in appearance from the female. He is sharply patterned black and white, while the female is a rich russet colour on the upperparts. The bird has a large, hooked bill and uses this to tackle all manner of insect prey.

94

Barred Antshrike *Thamnophilus doliatus* 16.5cm

Of all the antbirds this species is the most likely to be seen, as it can be found in a number of different habitats, such as forest edge, woodland, scrub, parks and gardens – anywhere, in fact, where there is some shrubbery in which to occasionally skulk and, of course, in which to nest. It is one of the most widespread and ubiquitous antshrikes in Ecuador and much of South America, except the temperate south. Its unique song is often heard – a series of accelerating and increasingly emphasized, semi-musical, nasal notes uttered by the male (depicted) and normally answered immediately by the female, which is usually close by. The song can perhaps be described thus: '*ah ah ah ah ah ahahahahahahah aahh*'. Both sexes are crested, and the female is rufous above and buff below.

Vaughan Ashby

Warbling Antbird *Hypocnemis cantator* 12cm

This species would be better named the Snarling Antbird, because its song certainly cannot be described as warbling. In fact, it has a distinctive voice – a series of rasping notes descending in scale. It has a distinguishing streaky black and white appearance, with contrasting rusty flanks. A common bird of the eastern lowlands, where it inhabits all manner of wooded habitats, it is more common in places such as successional growth and marginal areas along rivers, secondary growth and forest edge. It thrives in such areas, which are largely shunned by other antbirds that are more restricted to strictly forest habitats.

Ron Hoff

95

Amazonian Streaked Antwren
Myrmotherula multostriata 9.5cm

An uncommon antwren of the humid forests of the eastern low-lands of Ecuador, this species is locally more common in areas where its waterside habitat is prevalent. It is almost always only seen in vegetation beside streams and oxbow lakes, where its presence is usually only apparent when its characteristic lilting song is heard. This could perhaps be transcribed as '*pur-pee pur-pee pur-pee pur-pee*', wavering up and down the scale. Best seen from a small boat, the male is striped black and white, while the female has an attractive orange-rufous head finely streaked with black.

Chestnut-tailed Antbird *Myrmeciza hemimelaena* 12cm

In Ecuador this antbird is rare locally but has been recorded quite widely in the eastern lowland forests. It is perhaps less rare in the south. It is a bird of terra firma forest and can be seen near Kapawi Lodge on the Rio Pastaza. Birds occurring north of the Amazon, such as those in Ecuador, have a very different song from that of the population south of the Amazon, where the bird is also much more numerous. The Ecuadorian birds may be split as a separate and distinct species and called the White-bellied Antbird, *M. longipes*. This is a bird of the forest undergrowth and is often difficult to see, unless tape playback is used.

Silvered Antbird *Sclateria naevia* 14-14.5cm

Vaughan Ashby

A bird of stream sides, swampy forest and other wet places in the lowland forests of eastern Ecuador, this species it is rarely seen away from water. It is often seen from boats, when it is quite confiding, usually hopping in low vegetation just above the water or along the shore, with its tail slightly cocked. Its song is generally the first sign of its presence – it is loud and far carrying, starting with a single abrupt note closely followed by a fast, rising and accelerating series of notes. It is a very distinctive and commonly heard sound along the forested backwaters. The birds are usually grey above and white below with quite obvious long pink legs, with the female being browner above.

Giant Antpitta *Grallaria gigantea* 24-25cm

Eustace Barnes

Formerly belonging to the family Thamnophilidae, antpittas and anthrushes are now considered so different from antbirds that they warrant the status of a separate family, the Formicariidae. This magnificent member of a wonderful group of birds provides ample evidence for this move. It is an extraordinary and elusive ground-dweller that is very far removed in general appearance and habits from the true antbirds. Largely terrestrial and usually solitary, it takes great, leaping bounds, but can also run at great speed. It has been realized in recent years that this target bird for serious birders will venture out of the forest and come to food that has been provided, usually at dawn.

97

Chestnut-crowned Antpitta
Grallaria ruficapilla 19.5-20.5cm

Unlike the Giant Antpitta, *G. gigantea*, this species is common in the highlands of Ecuador at about 1,900–3,100m. Typically for an antpitta, it is especially short tailed and very long legged, and it is one of the most often seen species, occasionally venturing into the open in the early morning and late evening. Although it is generally shy, it can be bold and opportunistic – the author observed one bird that habitually loitered in the undergrowth behind a mobile burger bar at the side of a forest road, waiting for the stale buns and meat scraps to be tossed out. The species is very similar to Watkins's Antpitta, *G. watkinsi*, which is restricted to the south woodlands of Ecuador. It is not as likely to be seen in the open as the Tawny Antpitta, *G. quitensis*, which habitually forages above the tree line.

Jocotoco Antpitta *Grallaria ridgelyi* 23cm

Only recently discovered, this large and spectacular species has a very restricted range in southern Ecuador. It is a bird of dense forest (of which there are now only patches) with bamboo, on steep slopes at 2,300–2,650m. It is only slightly smaller than the Giant Antpitta, *G. gigantea*. Shy and wary, it is a difficult bird to see but can be heard in the breeding season, mainly at dawn and dusk, when its call is easily recognized, a hollow '*hoo, hoo, hoo…*' that is like the sound of a distant barking dog, hence its local name, *paquero perro*, or 'dog bird'. Some of its fragmented habitat has been protected from further destruction by the 'Jocotoco Foundation', and it may be seen (with luck) at the Tapichalaca Reserve/Honda Quebrada in Zamora-Chinchipe province.

Tropical Kingbird *Tyrannus melancholicus* 20cm

Vaughan Ashby

The Tropical Kingbird is one of the most common and most regularly encountered birds in the lowlands and lower Andean slopes both east and west. It shuns the drier areas of the west, as well as heavily forested areas except at borders and large clearings. It is a bird who's identity should be quickly learned because it a ubiquitous species, but it is easily recognized once learned. The Tropical Kingbird's profile when perched is upright and streamlined, and it often sits on telegraph wires, from where it sallies after its prey. The species is especially common in the months between April and September, when the southernmost migrant populations arrive to spend the austral winter in the warmer climes of the tropics. The bird is seen in both cities and the countryside, and has a distinctive, trilling call.

Great Kiskadee *Pitangus sulphuratus* 22cm

This is one of the largest and the most conspicuous of the yellow-breasted tyrant fly-catchers. The loud calls lend the species its name, '*kis-ka-dee*' or '*ven chee veee*', and they are one of the most characteristic and familiar sounds in many habitats all over Ecuador, except inside forest. The species occurs commonly in towns and villages, all manner of open areas and marginal habitats, and particularly likes areas near water. It is very easily recognized. Apart from the  bright yellow belly, its most obvious feature is the vibrant black and white head pattern. It has a heavy black bill and rufous margins on the wings and tail. It also has a semi-concealed yellow crown-stripe, which can flare in threat or display.

99

Boat-billed Flycatcher *Megarhynchus pitangua* 22–23cm

This species is superficially similar to – and only likely to be confused with – the much more common Great Kiskadee, *Pitangus sulphuratus*. However, with a good view it can be seen to have a heavier, much broader and deeper bill than the kiskadee, and a more curved upper mandible. The upperparts are generally more olive-hued and this species does not show much rufous on the closed wing. The bird has an especially characteristic nasal, gravelly, whining call that could be transcribed thus: '*yerg yerg yerg yerg*'. This call can be easily imitated and often results in the bird coming to investigate. The species is particularly fond of clearings, forest borders and riversides, so it is frequently seen from boats. Because it is quite arboreal, it rarely comes down to the ground like the Great Kiskadee.

Lesser Kiskadee *Philohydor lictor* 18cm

Vaughan Ashby

This smaller relative of the Great Kiskadee, *Pitangus sulphuratus*, is a slight and delicate bird in comparison. Although ostensibly similar in appearance, it is quite different in its habits. It is closely associated with waterside habitats, and is most often seen perched very low in aquatic vegetation along the edges of quiet forest backwaters and oxbow lakes. One of its most obvious physical distinctions is its long and seemingly narrow bill, which is vastly different from the robust bill of its greater cousin. It does not make the loud calls so typical of that bird, and its voice is quiet and anonymous – this considerably more specialized cousin will never be heard shouting '*kis-ka-dee*' from the rooftops.

Crowned Slaty Flycatcher
Griseotyrannus aurantioatrocristatus 18cm

birdholidays.co.uk

Displaying no bright colours or striking patterns except, as its name indicates, a distinguishing head pattern, this is a relatively anonymous member of the tyrant flycatcher family. The head pattern consists of a semi-concealed yellow coronal stripe bordered with black, which is difficult to see in the field. The bird migrates long distances from southern Brazil and Argentina to the eastern lowland rainforests of Ecuador during the southern winter months. The individual pictured was photographed when it landed on a ship during migration. In the austral winter the bird often lives in the tops of the highest forest trees and is habitually only seen well from canopy towers. It is perhaps most remarkable for having the longest binomial scientific name of any bird, extending to 33 letters!

Northern Tufted-Flycatcher
Mitrephanes phaeocercus 12cm

Found in the lower north-western foothills of the Andes up to about 600m, this is a fairly recent 'split' from what was formerly known as the Common Tufted-Flycatcher. Always typified by the pointed crest, this pretty flycatcher has the appearance of the pewees of the genus *Contopus*, and like them it often sallies to catch insects from a favourite perch and returns to that same perch, quivering its tail upon landing. It always shows an attractive warm buffy tone to the breast and a yellowish belly. Frequently seen in pairs at relatively low levels, it tends to remain in a particular area rather than moving with mixed species bird flocks. It utters short, high-pitched 'peeping' calls.

Cinnamon Flycatcher *Pyrrhomyias cinnamomeus* 13cm

Vaughan Ashby

A common and attractive little flycatcher, this is also a tame and confiding creature. It is familiar to many local people plying the mountain trails of Ecuador with their mules, and is very much at home along the man-made cuttings in the forest, in which it has space to sally after its insect prey and at times seems to simply ignore the presence of people. Its trilling call is also a common sound. Its endearing nature must make it a much-loved bird by the mountain communities, and while it is known by the pretty name of *mosquerito canelo* in Spanish, it no doubt has other names in the local languages of the various mountain people. It can be found at up to about 3,000m elevation.

Ruddy-tailed Flycatcher *Terenotriccus erythrurus* 10cm

Vaughan Ashby

This pretty flycatcher is quite common in the understorey of forest in the lowlands, both east and west of the Andes. As its common name suggests, it is characterized by its contrasting rufous tail. It also has particularly long and obvious rictal bristles, which help it to capture insects, generally from foliage during short sallies. It sometimes flicks one or both wings up over its back. It is usually seen singly but occasionally joins mixed species flocks, and is rather similar to the Cinnamon Neopipo, *Neopipo cinnamomea* (also known as the Cinnamon Tyrant), which is a much rarer inhabitant of Ecuador's eastern lowland forest.

Dusky-capped Flycatcher *Myiarchus tuberculifer* 17cm

This is just one of several members of the very confusing genus *Myiarchus*, consisting of relatively large members of the family of tyrant flycatchers, the Tyrannidae. It is not, however, as similar to other members of the genus as some of the species are. It can be separated by its very dark crown, which is normally quite apparent and can be almost black. This variably contrasts with the paler olive-brown mantle. The flight feathers are indistinctly edged with rufous. The Dusky-capped Flycatcher occurs on both slopes of the

Vaughan Ashby

Andes, but at much higher elevations in shrubbery on the Pacific slope. On the eastern Andean slope it occurs in forest-edge and semi-wooded habitats at up to about 1,800m.

Galapagos Flycatcher *Myiarchus magnirostris* 16cm

Also known as the Large-billed Flycatcher, this very small member of the *Myiarchus* genus is a common and obvious bird on the Galapagos Islands, occuring on all of the islands except Darwin, Wolf and Genovesa. It can sometimes be confused with the female Vermilion Flycatcher, *Pyrocephalus rubinus*. It has a large head, two very obvious wing-bars and a pale yellow belly, which is very typical of the family. However, it does not appear to have a particularly large bill, which

birdholidays.co.uk

belies its alternate common English name. As a flycatcher, it naturally enjoys areas containing bushes and trees from which it can sally for its insect prey.

Vermilion Flycatcher *Pyrocephalus rubinus* 13-15cm

This is a conspicuous and widespread bird on the Galapagos Islands, occurring on all the main islands, chiefly at higher altitudes. In continental Ecuador it is a common bird of the arid Pacific lowlands and slopes at up to about 3,000m locally. It is also an uncommon migrant to the eastern lowlands during the austral winter. It can often be seen in town parks and around homes and gardens,

Vaughan Ashby

where it can be very tame and approachable. The male has a bright red crown and underparts, and contrasting dark brown upperparts. The female is pale below with varying amounts of pink and sometimes yellow on the lower belly and vent, and usually some streaking on the breast.

Yellow-bellied Elaenia *Elaenia flavogaster* 16cm

Vaughan Ashby

One of eight species in this genus in Ecuador, this is a widespread bird of the western lowlands that is found in a variety of habitats. Its call, which has a fuzzy quality best transcribed as 'Breeer', is often heard but not recognized. Species in the *Elaenia* genus are notoriously hard to identify, even by experienced ornithologists. Although a member of the flycatcher family, this bird is by no means obliged to live only on insects and is sometimes found raiding fruiting trees in quite large numbers, particularly outside the breeding season.

104

Masked Water Tyrant *Fluvicola nengeta* 15cm

This sprightly little terrestrial flycatcher is a common bird near water in the western lowlands of Ecuador. Always on the move, fly-catching from the ground or rapidly chasing insect prey, it is an endearing bird with a crisp black and white plumage and a confiding nature. It is always found in the vicinity of water – a marsh or the edge of a rice field, a small stream or larger river, a park pond or even a swimming pool. It is absent from most of the interior of South America but reappears in eastern Brazil. The bird depicted is threatening its own reflection in a car window and wing mirror – an extreme example of the normal display of this species.

Common Tody-Flycatcher *Todirostrum cinereum* 9.5cm

As its name suggests, this is the most common and most often seen member of the tody-flycatchers, a group dominated by contrastingly plumaged little birds that usually display yellow underparts demarcated with darker grey or black upperparts. Although it is less ornate than some, this is nonetheless an especially attractive bird. Extremely active, it is an endearing species that is usually seen hopping about in the branches of its arboreal habitat with its tail cocked. It vocalizes frequently, giving 'ticking' or short 'trilling' notes. It is common on both sides of the Andes and is more widespread in the western lowlands, but somewhat inexplicably restricted to the foothills on the eastern flanks of the mountains.

Vaughan Ashby

105

Yellow-olive Flycatcher
Tolmomyias sulphurescens 14cm

As a member of the *Tolmomyias* genus, this bird has a typically broad-based bill. This group of flycatchers is also now known as flatbills, although there is already a different group under this label – the even broader and flatter billed members of the genus *Rynchocyclus*. This species is one of the most widespread members of the *Tolmomyias* genus, found in a variety of wooded habitats throughout Ecuador. Five other species in this genus are found in Ecuador, including the only recently described Orange-eyed Flatbill, *T. traylori*, from the eastern lowlands, which is poorly known but can be seen near Kapawi Lodge on the Pastaza River. The identification of the group of birds is difficult and complex, and birders are advised to consult *The Birds of South America* (Ridgely and Tudor) for more information.

White-throated Spadebill *Platyrinchus mystaceus* 9.5cm

birdholidays.co.uk

This tiny, stub-tailed and large-headed member of the flycatcher family is difficult to spot as it often sits for some time on the same perch. However, once located, it is not particularly shy and tends to perch in fairly open places within its preferred dense forest habitat. It is also likely to betray its presence with its penetrating high-pitched call, which is typically a sharp '*squeep*' that is sometimes repeated several times. When the bird flies to its next perch it is very difficult to follow and re-locate. It is easily recognized by its diagnostic facial pattern and very broad, laterally compressed bill. This is not obvious at certain angles, for example when the bird is seen side on (depicted).

106

Sepia-capped Flycatcher
Leptopogon amaurocephalus 13.5cm

This scarce and local member of the tyrant flycatcher clan is found in lower growth of the lowland forests of eastern Ecuador. As a *Leptopogon* it has several quite distinctive traits (for a flycatcher), which give the observer clues to its identity. Firstly, members of this group are usually long and slim and have rather narrow bills, which sets them

Phil Palmer

apart from the 'flat-billed' *Tolmomyius* group in particular. They also habitually flick a wing up over their back. In this species the cap is actually dark brown rather than 'sepia', and the bird's most distinctive feature is probably the dark patch on the ear-coverts. The closely related and considerably more common Slaty-capped Flycatcher, *L. superciliaris*, has a slate-grey crown and is a bird of the higher subtropical elevations.

Torrent Tyrannulet *Serpophaga cinerea* 11.5cm

Vaughan Ashby

A common and noticeable bird of the fast-flowing mountain streams that are such a predominant feature of the Ecuadorian highlands, this species occurs at altitudes of about 700–3,100m. It is mostly grey, blacker on the wings, head and tail, and paler below, and has narrow, paler wing-bars. It sallies in the air or vegetation to capture insect prey. Its song is a series of sharp '*sip*' or '*chip*' notes, which are designed to be heard over the rushing torrent, as is usual for birds living in this noisy environment. Pairs are often seen perched fairly close to each other, either on rocks in mid-stream or on banks. This species is unlikely to be mistaken for any other bird in its chosen watery niche.

Long-tailed Tyrant *Colonia colonus* 17–29cm

Phil Palmer

The wide range in the measurements of this species relates to the elongated central tail feathers of the adult which may be up to 12cm longer than the rest of the tail. With their overall black plumage, near-white crown and unique tail, the adults are unmistakable. They are often seen in pairs. The female is similar to the male but has shorter tail feathers. This is also a very predictable bird, remaining loyal to a few favoured perches over a long period. These are nearly always high, unobscured snags or the tips of *Cecropia* tree shoots, where the bird is extremely obvious.

White-banded Tyrannulet
Mecocerculus stictopterus 12.5cm

birdholidays.co.uk

With its bold white supercilium and wing-bars, this is one of the most easily recognized members of the tyrannulet tribe. Quite large and rather long-tailed, this attractive and generally common flycatcher is a bird of woodland and cloud forest on both slopes of the Andes at about 2,400–3,500m elevation – that is, all the way up to the tree line, and even into the polylepis scrub beyond. It is quite vocal, often giving a rasping '*squeeeh*' call, which sometimes runs into a repeated trill. This bird readily joins mixed species flocks, where it is usually very obvious as it perches in the open and actively gleans from foliage. It will often otherwise be seen foraging alone or as a pair.

Páramo Ground Tyrant *Muscisaxicola alpinus* 19cm

birdholidays.co.uk

Previously considered to be a race of the Plain-capped Ground Tyrant, *M. grisea*, of the highlands of Peru and Bolivia, this bird has now been afforded full species status. It occurs singly or in pairs in open terrain at very high elevations of about 3,800–4,600m, far above the tree line, and never seeks cover. Instead it relies on its fast flight to escape unwanted attention. Outside the breeding season it might be seen in small flocks. It can be confused with the migrant White-browed Ground Tyrant, *M. albilora*, but that species never shows as much white in front of the eye. It often flies long distances from one area to another on its long, pointed wings, forages on the ground and stands with an upright stance in the manner of the wheatears of Europe and Asia.

White-winged Becard
Pachyramphus polychopterus 14.5–15cm

Phil Palmer

A bird of the eastern lowlands, this species is found in a variety of wooded habitats including gallery forest, Várzea, forest borders, more open secondary woodland and plantations. Of the 12 species of becard in Ecuador, this is the most variable. Some subspecies are quite pale grey below with a black cap, but the form shown (*P. p. tenebrosus*) is the blackest and glossiest. All subspecies have large white wing-bars and variable amounts of white on the shoulder. Although they are members of the tyrant flycatcher family, the becards tend to be slow moving and this species is also very tame.

Spangled Cotinga *Cotinga cayana* 20cm

This particularly beautiful cotinga is most often seen from canopy observation towers as it spends its entire time roaming through the rainforest treetops from one fruiting tree to another. It is also most easily seen in the early morning sunshine, when it perches out in the open and basks before setting off to forage. As a fruit eater it does not have to be up too early because it knows most of the fruit will probably still be there and will be riper later. However, if an influx of migrant Eastern Kingbirds, *Tyrranus tyrranus*, occurs, a regular food source can be stripped of fruit in a very short time. Fortunately for the Spangled Cotinga, the kingbirds are usually on passage to their wintering areas in Peru.

Purple-throated Fruitcrow *Querula purpurata* 28–30cm

This large member of the cotinga family is fairly widespread in the lowland forests of eastern Ecuador. As a fruit eater, it wanders around high in the forest canopy in loose flocks, foraging from various trees, but is nearly always first encountered when you hear its distinctive, soft, far-carrying mewing calls, perhaps best transcribed as '*pew...pew*'. It has a gentle, loping flight action. Its name is entirely descriptive – it is a crow-like bird with an entirely blackish plumage except for a lovely purple throat, although this can be hard to see in poor light. The female lacks this adornment, being uniform black in colour.

Andean Cock-of-the-Rock *Rupicola peruvianus* 30cm

Vaughan Ashby

One of the most iconic and easily recognized birds of Ecuador, this is a species of the cloud forests of both the eastern and western Andean slopes. The bird pictured is a male from the eastern slope – birds on the western slope are a deeper reddish-orange. A member of the cotinga family, this bird is known for its strange, cat-like calls, which indicate the presence of a lek, where the males gather to display in the hope of attracting a mate. Unless you see a flash of brilliant tangerine zooming past or are fortunate enough to encounter these fabulous birds at a fruiting tree, the leks are where birders have the best chance of seeing them. These noisy gatherings involve males bowing and wing-flapping to attract attention and are a spectacle not to be missed.

White-browed Purpletuft *Iodopleura isabellae* 11.5cm

Eustace Barnes

An uncommon and quite strange little bird found in the forested eastern lowlands, this is one of the smallest species in the cotinga family. Although it is generally a fruit eater, it is probably most frequently seen perched on a bare branch, which serves as a post from which it sallies after insects. It is often overlooked as it is so small and sometimes sits quietly for long periods. As its name suggests, it does indeed have 'purple tufts', but these are usually hidden under the wing. This species builds a minute lichen nest (depicted) on a bare limb to accommodate a single tiny chick, which relies on its camouflage to survive. The chick (shown at the top of the picture) remains frozen for much of the time in the fashion of a potoo, simply pretending to be a piece of the branch. This is perhaps the first time a photograph of this species and its nest has been published.

111

Black-chested Fruiteater *Pipreola lubomirskii* 18cm

This member of the cotinga family is a scarce bird of the subtropical forest of the eastern Andean slope at elevations of 1,500–2,100m. The male is typically handsome, with a glossy black head and throat contrasting with bright green upperparts and a yellow belly. This fabulous combination is further offset by a bright yellow iris and a coral-red bill. The female is a uniform green with a pale yellow belly that is streaked with green. The bird is often heard rather

than seen, but its call must first be recognized – a thin, ascending, high-pitched note, '*pseeeeeeeeeeeeeeet*', which can be difficult for some people to even hear. This species is best observed when found at a fruiting tree.

Orange-breasted Fruiteater *Pipreola jucunda* 18cm

This particular fruiteater is a bird of the western Andean slope, where it is unmistakable. It is principally found in mossy subtropical cloud forest at 600–1,700m. Like many members of the strange cotinga family, it is an uncommon and enigmatic bird, although there are few opportunities to access its steep forested habitat to assess its true status. The male's plumage is spectacular: the black head, red bill and yellow iris are quite typical of the genus, but this bird is then further

adorned with a blazing orange breast extending to the sides of the neck. Its thin, high-pitched call is very similar to that of the previous species. The female is, as is usual in this group of birds, far more uniform green and streaked below.

112

Golden-headed Manakin *Pipra erythrocephala* 9cm

This is a typically impressive manakin, which occurs in the lowland forest east of the Andes. Its main feature is the male's brilliant golden-yellow head, contrasting with the uniform black of the rest of the bird's plumage. The male also has startling red and white thighs, which although exposed when displaying are otherwise usually concealed. As is usual in manakins, the female is a drab creature compared with the male – a uniform olive colour with a paler belly and pale bill. Displays by this species at leks are noisy and flashy affairs, with the males trilling and buzzing. The bird is most commonly seen near fruiting trees.

White-bearded Manakin *Manacus manacus* 11cm

This tiny member of the cotinga family is distinguished by its behaviour at leks, which involves a great deal of calling and noisy wing-snapping. The wings are used to make the very loud cracking noises that make the bird's leks so peculiar and obvious. At the same time, the males stick out their throat feathers to form something like a 'flag', or the 'beard' that gives the bird its name. With a black back and cap, and a white collar and underparts, the male is very dapper. The female is an olive-green bird, her most obvious feature being her bright orange legs, also a feature of the male.

113

Blue-backed Manakin *Chiroxiphia pareola* 12.5cm

A very attractive bird of the eastern lowlands of Ecuador, this manakin is found in the lower levels of terra firma forest. Within its range, the red-crowned and blue-backed black male is unmistakable, but the female is far more difficult to identify. She is very similar to other female manakins but is not found in the same habitat and is generally a bird of secondary woodland. She most closely resembles the female Green Manakin, *Xenopipo holochlora*, but in that species the female has dark legs. This species has a varied vocabulary and the males perform complex 'dances' to attract their potential mates.

Cinereous Mourner *Laniocera hypopyrra* 20cm

This is an unusual member of the tyrant flycatcher family. At first glance it appears to be just an anonymous grey bird, but with good views it can be seen to have two lines of cinnamon-coloured spots on the wings. These spotted wing-bars are formed by the tips to the lesser and median coverts. The tertials and tail feathers are also tipped with the same contrasting colour. This generally scarce and inconspicuous bird is found in the lowlands of the east in the middle storey of terra firma forest. Young birds are difficult to identify – they have a rufous- and black-spotted pattern on the breast. The species' song is a repeated series of high-pitched, ringing calls

Long-tailed Mockingbird *Mimus longicaudatus* 29cm

This is one of the most common and conspicuous birds of Ecuador's western lowlands, coast and mountain slopes (occasionally recorded at nearly 2,000m). There are only two Mimidae members in mainland Ecuador (although there are several other species on the Galapagos Islands). The other continental species is the Tropical Mockingbird, *M. gilvus*, which is rare and local in the north, and has only recently been found in Ecuador. The Long-tailed Mockingbird is a tame and very familiar bird. It is very recognizable by its long, white-tipped tail, which is often swung about or held aloft in a vertical position. Often active throughout the day, it runs and hops on the ground on its long, strong legs, but does not usually fly very far. As its scientific name suggests, it is an accomplished songster and mimic.

Galapagos Mockingbird *Nesomimus parvulus* 25cm

This is the most widespread of the mockingbirds of the Galapagos archipelago, with no less than six subspecies scattered across a number of islands. Its range does not overlap with any of the other three species that occur on the islands, however. Its loud and melodious voice is a common sound. Unlike most other 'mockers', this species does not have a distinct malar stripe, but has an iris colour that varies from reddish-brown to yellowish-green. It is otherwise very similar to the Floreana or Charles Mockingbird, *N. trifasciatus*, which is only found on two islands and classified as Endangered, and has a total population of just 150 birds. The San Cristobal or Chatham Mockingbird, *N. melanotis*, is another Galapagos endemic, only found on San Cristobal Island; however, unlike its relative on Floreana Island, it is common here.

115

Hooded Mockingbird *Nesomimus macdonaldi* 28cm

This large and mostly terrestrial mockingbird is well known for being remarkably tame, even landing on people with a view to using them as mobile perches or just to raid their packed lunches. Its lifestyle demands that it has long, strong legs as it rarely flies, preferring to run. It also has a long and strongly decurved bill. It is common on the Galapagos Islands of Española and Gardner-by-Española. During the breeding season it has a loud and strident song. Outside the breeding season it may gather in roving and sometimes slightly intimidating flocks. It looks similar to the Galapagos Mockingbird, *N. parvulus*, but is more heavily streaked and has a distinct malar stripe and an obvious pale collar.

Black-capped Donacobius *Donacobius atricapilla* 22cm

This handsome bird inhabits marshy habitats in the eastern lowlands of Ecuador, in particular the wet grassy margins of oxbow lakes where it is widespread and relatively common. It is distinctive due to its dapper combination of rich brown upperparts and bright creamy-buff underparts, and a long black tail with flashy white tips. This pattern is set off by a black head and gleaming yellow eye. The bird often gives away its presence by its loud, ringing calls. Although quite inconspicuous when foraging in dense vegetation, it also sits up in prominent places to call, swinging its tail about to show off the white tips.

Southern House Wren *Troglodytes aedon* 11.5cm

The song of this wren – one of the most ubiquitous birds of the Americas – can be heard from Alaska to Tierra del Fuego. In Ecuador (which is more or less right in the middle of its latitudinal range), this song can be heard from sea level to the tree line, and even above it. This species is very opportunistic and clever, well-known traits in wrens. The concrete

Vaughan Ashby

'jungles' of the highlands are as likely to have a population of Southern House Wrens as a clearing in the real lowland jungles of Ecuador. The birds can be seen and heard in parks, gardens, forest edge and agricultural areas, and on the beach – in fact anywhere except the highest Páramo (unless it is an area containing houses) and the interior of lowland rainforest (unless it is a clearing).

Thrush-like Wren *Campylorhynchus turdinus* 20.5cm

This large and conspicuous wren has one of the most remarkable and memorable songs of any Ecuadorian bird. No other bird has a similar voice, and its loud, explosive, carolling series of liquid, melodic notes delivered as a duet is absolutely unique. It is a commonly heard sound in the forests and forest borders of the eastern lowlands, and the bird itself is generally a common sight around the clearings and gardens of the lodges and hotels that are such a useful feature of the area. The subspecies that occurs in Ecuador is the Amazonian race, *C. t. hypostistcus*, which is very heavily spotted below. The unspotted southern race is depicted here.

117

Chiguanco Thrush *Turdus chiguanco* 27.5cm

Vaughan Ashby

This is one of the most obvious birds in the towns and cities of the highlands of Ecuador, especially in the parks and gardens. It is also a common feature of a variety of environments in the countryside, and is most common in semi-wooded habitats. It is very likely to be encountered almost anywhere above about 1,500m until you reach the tree line. Its song is not the most exciting of thrush songs, being rather simple and repetitive. However, it is often heard in the early morning and late evening, and is a familiar background sound in many cities that offsets, to a degree, the modern and even more familiar sound of traffic. Like most common and plain birds, this species of thrush is enjoyed by the many rather than the few.

Great Thrush *Turdus fuscater* 33cm

birdholidays.co.uk

A very common feature of the avian landscape of the highlands, this thrush can be seen in almost any semi-open habitats up to the tree line, except very arid areas. It is a familiar bird in town parks, gardens and agricultural areas, and is superficially similar to its smaller relative, the Chiguanco Thrush, *T. chiguanco*, but that bird is considerably smaller and paler. The Great Thrush is very conspicuous, being so large, black and common. Birds in Azuay province and further south, however, are paler and more closely resemble the Chiguanco in colour. The male in breeding plumage has a bright orange bill and a bright yellow eye-ring. The female lacks the eye-ring at all times. This species utters loud calls, but has a sweet, rather subdued song.

Grey-breasted Martin *Progne chalybea* 19cm

A large and common martin in most parts of its range, this species is loud, conspicuous and inquisitive, and is one of the birds that is most obvious around towns and villages. It often flies out from the banks of the lowland rivers to investigate and land on boats, calling excitedly with its rich, churring or chuckling sound. The male is deep blue above and white below with a grey breast. The female is brown above and pale below with a rather darker breast and throat. The Brown-chested Martin, *P. tapera*, is similar, but has a pale throat and is always brown above. Like all members of the swallow family, this is usually a bird that is very much accepted, welcomed and largely enjoyed as a member of the community.

Brown-chested Martin *Progne tapera* 18cm

This large martin is a lot less common than the Grey-breasted Martin, *P. chalybea*, but is found in similar habitats and can be confused with it when both species are in the same place at the same time, particularly because its call is very similar. Grey-breasted Martins, however, are always blue-black above, whereas this species is always brown above. The only similarly plumaged member of the family in Ecuador is the considerably smaller Sand Martin, *Riparia riparia*, which is a migrant from the north. It soars gracefully and flashes white on the outer tail. In the eastern lowlands of Ecuador, this bird arrives as an austral migrant from the south to swell the numbers of the local population. In the south-west it is a common resident.

119

Southern Roughwing *Stelgidopteryx ruficollis* 13 cm

One of the most commonly encountered swallows in the lowlands of the east and west of Ecuador up to an elevation of about 1,000m, this is not a colourful bird, but it is quite distinctive in its sleek shape. It has long wings and a style of flight that is strong, fast and elegant. It is generally a dull-brown colour, with a brighter and paler rump and underparts, and a rather warmer cinnamon-buff throat. It is often seen over water and nests in riverbanks, also burrowing into road cuts, like many other swallow species, making good use of the presence of humans. Its loud '*jreeep*' call is familiar along the banks of the lowland waterways.

White-winged Swallow *Tachycineta albiventer* 13.5 cm

This beautiful swallow is closely associated with the rivers, oxbow lakes and marshy areas of Ecuador. Many dwellings sited alongside rivers have installed purpose-built houses for this species, and it readily takes advantage of these nesting opportunities. It is most frequently observed foraging over water, frequently flying very close to the surface. When it is seen perched, it is almost always on branches of

submerged trees or fishermen's marker posts protruding above the water's surface. The turquoise-green upperparts, gleaming white underside and white fringes to the inner feathers on the upper wing are diagnostic. Young birds may lack these features, however, and are much browner above. This species is usually very confiding.

Blue-and-white Swallow
Notiochelidon cyanoleuca 12.5cm

Deep glossy blue above and white below, with contrasting black under-tail coverts, this is an endearing and pretty lit-tle swallow, which often lives in close proximity to humans. It is thus a conspicuous and famil-iar bird in Ecuador's countryside in general, including urban areas. A widespread swallow in the highlands, it can be found hawking over any habitat. Nesting appears to more or less depend on the availability of crevices, and just about anything that has a hole in it appears to be suitable. The resident population in the eastern lowlands is joined by a few migrants from the southern populations during the aus-tral winter months (April–September).

Slate-throated Redstart *Myioborus miniatus* 13cm

Vaughan Ashby

This is a common and appealing bird of the cloud forests of the subtropical eastern Andean slope at about 800–2,400m. Recently renamed the Slate-throated Whitestart, it does indeed flash its white outer tail feathers, and the alternative name reflects this fea-ture. I retain its original common name here as this is what it has traditionally been called (even though it does not have any red in its tail at all). This member of the Parulidae is closely related to the migrant American Redstart, *Setophaga ruticilla*, named by the first English colonists to the New World – this bird visits Ecuador in small numbers during the northern winter months, and shows red, orange or yellow in its tail. It frequently forages with drooping wings and a cocked tail.

121

Yellow Warbler *Dendroica petechia* 12cm

The taxonomy of this group of warblers is complex in Ecuador. The race *D. p. aureola* is classed as near endemic to the Galapagos archipelago, as it is also found on the Cocos Islands. This is the race illustrated here. The race *D. p. aestiva* is an uncommon visitor to the lowlands of the mainland during the boreal winter. The nominate race *D. p. petechia* has been 'split' by some authorities and is known by the English name of Mangrove Warbler, as mangrove forest is its favoured habitat along the mainland coast; it is still a relatively common bird where this endangered habitat remains.

Large Cactus Finch *Geospiza conirostris* 15cm

Endemic to the Galapagos Islands and one of the birds famously described by Charles Darwin in his studies while working as a naturalist aboard HMS *Beagle*, this species features prominently in his thesis on the theory of evolution. This bird is dependent on *Opuntia* cacti (otherwise known as prickly pears) as a food source. It is far more restricted in its range than the more widespread Cactus Finch, *G. scandens*, and breeds only on the islands of Española (subspecies *G. c. conirostris*) Darwin and Wolf (subspecies *G. c. darwinii*), and Genovesa (subspecies *G. c. propinqua*).

Warbler Finch *Certhidia olivacea* 10cm

Endemic to the Galapagos Islands, this is just one member of the remarkably diverse 'Darwin's finches' family – birds that were originally thought to belong in the family Emberizinae (the buntings and sparrows). Recent work involving DNI analysis has shown them to in fact be related to the tanager family, the Thraupinae. This species has a very specialized bill adaptation, as suggested by its common name. The bill is slender and pointed, making the bird look remarkably like a warbler or small tanager. The smallest of all of Darwin's finches, the Warbler Finch is common and widespread on the Galapagos Islands wherever there is vegetation.

Large Ground-Finch *Geospiza magnirostris* 16cm

The Large Ground-Finch uses its massive bill to crack open the tough outer layers of certain seeds and the eggs of other birds, on which it sometimes feeds. It inhabits the dry forest and shrub land of most of the larger islands. Like all but one member of the Thraupidae subfamily known as Darwin's finches, it is endemic to the Galapagos Islands, and thus, politically, Ecuador too. The only member of the Darwin's finch group that is not endemic to Ecuador is the Cocos Finch, *Pinaroloxias inornata*. It occurs only on the island of Cocos, which lies 360 miles off Costa Rica's coast.

Medium Ground-Finch *Geospiza fortis* 12.5cm

This, the smaller relative of the Large Ground-Finch, *G. magnirostris*, is a member of the subfamily of the tanagers (Thraupinae) known as Darwin's finches. Like its larger congener, it is a bird of the dry scrubby forest. It is common and widespread across the Galapagos Islands and is, of course, found nowhere else. It is just one of this remarkable group of birds that have become highly adapted to their environment and have, in particular, specialized bills that provide them with the ability to exploit a specific ecological niche in that environment. Studies show that at the time when its larger relative arrived on the island of Daphne, this species evolved within just two decades, reducing its bill size to more effectively exploit different food sources.

Small Tree-Finch *Camarynchus parvulus* 11cm

Endemic to the Galapagos Islands, this widespread and short-tailed member of the family is represented by two different subspecies, the race *C. p. salvini* being restricted to the island of San Cristobal. As its name clearly suggests, this is the smallest of the tree-finches. It resembles a tit or chickadee in its feeding manner, sometimes hanging upside down while gleaning from small branches. The female is relatively nondescript, and lacks the male's dark head. The species has a rather small and stubby bill, which it uses to forage on the ground at times. It is most common in the highlands, but can also be seen in the arid zone.

Vegetarian Finch *Camarhynchus crassirostris* 16cm

This large bird is another uniquely adapted member of the Darwin's finches that are endemic to the Galapagos Islands. Although generally uncommon, it is found on all the main islands. Its preferred habitat is in the 'transition zone' at moderate elevations, but it may sometimes be found in the higher, wetter zone or the more arid scrublands at lower elevations. It has a somewhat different song from the songs of the other tree-finches in this genus – loud and musical, followed by a harsh buzzing note and perhaps ending with a whistled note.

Small Ground-Finch *Geospiza fuliginosa* 11cm

This species of ground-finch is endemic to the Galapagos Islands and is an opportunistic member of the clan. As well as eating seeds and other vegetable matter, it feeds on mites and ticks found on giant tortoises and both marine and land iguanas. In doing so, it provides a kind of health service to them. This species is very similar to the next one, but does not share its habit of pecking at nesting boobies to sup on their blood! Other ground-finch species have equally amazing behaviour: one species, the Woodpecker Finch, *Camarhynchus pallidus*, is a specialized tool user that habitually uses a small twig to prise food from nooks and crannies in trees, and even carries a particularly effective piece of equipment for some time.

125

Sharp-beaked Ground-Finch *Geospiza difficilis* 12.5cm

birdholidays.co.uk

Endemic to the Galapagos Islands, this member of the ground-finch family is fairly common where it occurs, but it is patchily distributed on the islands. The Sharp-beaked Ground-Finches on the islands of Darwin and Wolf are well known for pecking at the skins of nesting boobies to make them bleed and then feeding on the blood – a habit that has resulted in this subpecies (*G. d. septentrionalis*) being given the common name of the Vampire Ground-Finch. This is just one pattern of behaviour that led Charles Darwin to conclude that this isolated population of birds was rapidly adapting to very specific circumstances, a hypothesis and concept that was later to become accepted as 'evolution'.

Bananaquit *Coereba flaveola* 11cm

A common little member of the tanager family, this nectivorous species is one of the birds most often seen raiding hummingbird feeders, often to the point of excluding the hummingbirds themselves. It normally feeds at fruiting trees, but commonly enters and sometimes nests inside homes, and will even eat marmalade from the toast on the breakfast plate when your back is turned. Because of its cheeky nature, this species is very familiar and its presence is enjoyed by many people. It is characterized by its striking plumage and short, decurved bill. There are several subspecies, some with longer bills than others.

126

Blue-naped Chlorophonia *Chlorophonia cyanea* 11.5cm

Male Female

This extraordinary-looking little bird is a resident of the eastern Andean slope at about 800–2,000m. It sometimes comes to feeders, but under 'normal' conditions feeds in fruiting trees. It is a mistletoe specialist in particular, and one of the birds that is so crucial in spreading and helping to propagate such an important resource for itself and other birds. Like many of its close relatives, it also very much enjoys feeding on *Cecropia* trees when they are in season. It can be inconspicuous and difficult to spot, as it is very capable of blending in with the foliage in which it forages.

Purple Honeycreeper *Cyanerpes caeruleus* 11cm

The male of this honeycreeper is unmistakable, having deep but bright bluish-purple body plumage, a contrasting black mask, wings and tail, and thick, bright yellow legs. The female is a greenish colour above and streaked below, with an orange-buff throat, blue malar stripe and duller greenish-yellow legs. Both sexes have slender decurved bills. This is a common member of roving flocks of tanagers in the eastern lowlands and lower Andean foothills, most often seen at fruiting trees, but also readily comes to feeders.

127

Green Honeycreeper *Chlorophanes spiza* 14cm

This is the largest of the Ecuadorian honeycreepers and the only one in which the male is bright shining turquoise-green rather than a shade of blue. The male also has a contrasting black mask, while the female is very different, being a uniform green. The bird commonly visits hummingbird feeders when not at its natural food sources of flowering or fruiting trees. In both sexes the slightly decurved bill shows a lot of yellow on the lower mandible and the base of the upper mandible, and the eye is red. This is a bird of lowland and lower foothill forest, clearings, borders and gardens.

Magpie Tanager *Cissopis leverianus* 26cm

This is a very large, conspicuous tanager that is hard to miss in its range. It has a dramatic black and white pattern and a long tail, and is very eye-catching. It is common in all types of forested, wooded and semi-wooded habitats in the eastern lowlands of Ecuador. It sometimes wanders up into the foothills, and has been recorded at up to about 1,200m elevation on the east Andean slope. However, it is most often seen in clearings, at the forest edge or perhaps flying across a river. It readily comes to feeders where fruit is provided. Magpie Tanagers are usually seen in pairs, or singly during the breeding season. They tend not to move with mixed species flocks.

Flame-crested Tanager *Tachyphonus cristatus* 16cm

This is a bird of the forests of the eastern lowlands of Ecuador, which very occasionally ventures into the foothills in places. It is generally a bird that stays fairly high in the trees. The somewhat bizarre plumage of the male is similar to that of its close relative, the Fulvous-crested Tanager, *T. surinamus*. However, that species is generally an inhabitant of the lower levels of the forest, and never shows a buff throat patch or the strange, flattened orange-red crest that gives this bird its name.

Phil Palmer

As is usual in this group of tanagers, the female is very different from the male. In this species she is brown and rufous, while her relative shows more olive tones and a greyer head.

Swallow Tanager *Tersina viridis* 15cm

Phil Palmer

Male

Female

This unusual and beautiful tanager is quite prevalent in the lowlands on both sides of the Andes. Either sex could easily be mistaken for some kind of cotinga due to the bird's habit of sitting out on open limbs. From these perches it sallies out to catch insects, much like the Swallow-winged Puffbird, *Chelidoptera tenebrosa*, with which it often shares its habitat. At other times it is partial to eating fruit, and can sometimes be found in some numbers at a single tree. The vivid blue male is very different from the dull greenish female. The species may be seen congregating in small parties, often along rivers, where it nests in holes burrowed into the banks.

Rufous-bellied Euphonia *Euphonia rufiventris* 11cm

This is just one of a remarkable total of ten species of Euphonia that occur in Ecuador. This particular species is an inhabitant of the humid lowlands east of the Andes, and in some places it can be found at up to about 500m elevation near the lower mountain slopes. Its habitat requirements are essentially tall forest. Being a strictly arboreal bird, this species is usually seen high in the trees, but also sometimes comes to feed in fruiting trees in the lower canopy or even the understorey. The main feature of its plumage that makes it distinct from other euphonias is the unusual lack of yellow on the forehead.

White-lored Euphonia *Euphonia chrysopasta* 11cm

This is a quite unusual euphonia as it does not present the graphic, glossy, purple-black and yellow pattern of most members of this group of little tanagers. Its main feature, setting it apart from the others, is the white patch in front of its eye. A bird of the lowland forests of eastern Ecuador, it is most likely to be seen fairly high up, at the forest edge. Inside the forest it may be rather anonymous, because it will normally only present its underparts to an observer revealing little to give away its identity. As is usual in the euphonias, it has an extensive repertoire of calls as well as an intricate song.

Highland Hepatic Tanager *Piranga lutea* 18cm

This is one of the most common members of the large and diverse tanager family, of which there are an incredible 143 species in Ecuador. Formerly simply regarded as just one species, the form *P. l. lutea* is now generally regarded to be a distinct species. Despite the bird's common name, indicating that it is a montane bird, it actually occurs most commonly in the coastal lowlands. On the east Andean slope it is generally most likely to be seen at about 1,000–1,400m elevation, and on the west slope it may be seen at up to 1,900m. The male's red plumage is distinctive, except for possible confusion with the Summer Tanager, *P. rubra*, an uncommon visitor in the northern winter months. That species has a darker and slightly longer bill, and is a paler shade of red. The female is much like the female Summer Tanager, but has a pale bill.

Silver-beaked Tanager *Ramphocelus carbo* 18cm

This is one of the most frequently encountered birds of urban and suburban areas, and secondary growth and other wooded habitats in the eastern lowlands, where it occurs in almost all gardens. The male is instantly recognizable by the silvery-white sides to his bill, and by his deep and rather beautiful maroon-red plumage, which often appears black when seen in poor light. The female also has the whitish sides to the bill, although they are less obvious than in the male. She is a rather uniform rusty-brown colour. Although this species is common and conspicuous, with a good view the male can be recognized as a really lovely bird.

131

Blue-grey Tanager *Thraupis episcopus* 16cm

This is one of the most regularly encountered and most conspicuous of Ecuadorian birds, and a common species in and around towns and villages on the west side of the Andes up to an elevation of about 1,500m. Like the Palm Tanager, *T. palmarum*, it is not found in primary forest but nearly always in parks, gardens, secondary growth and cultivated areas. It is easily recognized by its lovely blue and grey plumage. The subspecies from the eastern lowlands (depicted) has obvious white wing-bars, which are lacking on the more uniform birds from the western lowlands.

Palm Tanager *Thraupis palmarum* 18cm

This is one of the most common tanagers in the lowlands on both sides of the Andes, and also one of the most nondescript. It is often seen around human habitations, but occurs in a variety of habitats where there are trees of any type. As its name suggests, it has a preference for palms, but this is by no means a strict requirement – although it is most often seen as a rather nondescript bird flying into a palm tree! Its loud, high-pitched calls are a constant feature of parks and gardens. Its plumage is characterized by its generally plain appearance – a dull olive-grey with blackish flight feathers that give the bird a clear-cut bicoloured wing pattern.

Crested Oropendola *Psarocolius decumanus* 45cm

One of seven oropendola species in Ecuador, this is the only black-bodied one. It has a long and pointed, ivory-white bill and its crest is barely visible, being just a single filament. It is an extremely striking bird with brilliant yellow outer tail feathers, in common with other members of the group. Also in common with other oropendolas, it builds pendulous, hanging nests in conspicuous colonies. Very often these are in isolated trees in clearings or on riverbanks, well away from the forest edge, and where they are afforded protection from predation by monkeys. The birds are often seen flying across rivers in loose flocks en route to a food source or returning to the colony after a foray.

Giant Cowbird *Scaphidura oryzivora* 12–15 cm

An iridescent black-bird family member, this species is often seen from boats travelling along the waterways of the eastern lowlands, and is also common in the west. The males – which are much larger than the females – display by strutting on their long legs with inflated breasts, accentuating their large size. In flight this species has a distinctive powerful loping action. As is usual in the cowbirds,

it is a brood parasite and, as the largest of them all, parasitises oropendolas and caciques. The females can often be seen in the vicinity of a colony waiting for a chance to deposit an egg.

Phil Palmer

133

Red-breasted Blackbird *Sturnella militaris* 19cm

Perhaps better called a meadowlark, the male of this species is a spectacular bird with a bright red breast that is like no other in its range. It inhabits damp pastures in the eastern lowlands and, although it is relatively locally distributed, its population is certain to increase and spread as it takes advantage of increased deforestation in the region. It is inclined to gather in some numbers outside the breeding season. Typical of the blackbirds, the female is of a very different appearance from the male. She has a well-camouflaged pattern of streaky brown above, but usually with a variable tinge of pink or red below. The birds could be confused with the Bobolink, *Dolichonyx oryzivorus*, which arrives from the north during the winter months, but that species has a stubby pink bill rather than the pointed dark bill of this bird.

Troupial *Icterus icterus* 23cm

Also known as the Orange-backed Oriole, this fabulous bird deserves to be simply called the Troupial. A relatively common but spectacular member of the oriole family, it is found in a variety of habitats in the Oriente, or the eastern lowlands of Ecuador. It is best recognized by its fantastic appearance – bright tangerine-orange body plumage set off very sharply with a black throat, wings and tail, and a splash of white, just to add to the effect. No other bird looks like this and, once seen, it is never forgotten. It is perhaps the most extravagantly beautiful of the American oriole clan. It can, however, be remarkably inconspicuous despite its vivid colour, and is most often seen as a flash of colour as it flies across a road or river.

Green Jay *Cyanocorax yncas* 30cm

Eustace Barnes

This is one of the most distinctive members of this branch of the crow family, with a unique appearance. It roves in noisy flocks through the cloud forests of the eastern Andean slope at 1,300–2,200m, looking for anything edible. It is a lovely bird with a multi-patterned and colourful plumage. It has green upperparts, yellow underparts, a bluish-white head, and a black face and throat, adorned with a crested, vibrant blue forehead. The tail is green with contrasting yellow outer tail feathers. Although shy, the bird is also very inquisitive. Some authorities have recently split it from the northern form and have named it the Inca Jay.

Rufous-collared Sparrow *Zonotrichia capensis* 14cm

Perhaps the most ubiquitous small bird in the highlands of Ecuador, this species is found in all highland regions at above about 1,500m on the east Andean slope, and locally down to about 600m. It is replaced by the Yellow-browed Sparrow, *Ammodramus aurifrons*, in the humid eastern lowlands. It occurs in urban and rural areas alike, where its pretty, high-pitched, whistled song is heard almost constantly from dawn until dusk. The adult is very distinctive, with its rusty hind-neck, and grey head with black eye-stripes and sides of the peaked crown. The brown, streaky juveniles lack these features, but usually show some trace of the rusty collar.

135

Yellow-browed Sparrow *Ammodramus aurifrons* 13cm

In many ways this bird replaces the Rufous-collared Sparrow, *Zonotrichia capensis*, in marginal habitats and agricultural areas, such as pasture, at lower elevations east of the Andes up to about 1,300m. It is likely to be present anywhere where there are grassy areas. Not only is it a common bird in these areas, but its buzzy, trilling song is very frequently the birdsong most often heard from riverbanks. It sounds rather insect-like and can be heard even in the heat of the day, when most other birds have fallen silent. It is a somewhat nondescript small, streaky brown bird, but always has some degree of yellow on the head, usually on the lores, eye-ring and short supercilium.

Plain-coloured Seedeater *Catamenia inornata* 13.5cm

As its scientific name suggests, this little bird is rather less than ornate. Although the male is principally uniform grey, he has a pale pink bill and rich rufous undertail coverts, as the picture shows well. The female is a streakier bird and, as is usual in the seedeater family, generally outnumbers adult males. A group will often contain up to about six or more brown and streaky females and juveniles, which may be difficult to put a name to until the male makes an appearance. This is a bird of the highlands at 2,600–3,800m. It is found in grassy places and Páramo, and typically forages on or close to the ground.

Vaughan Ashby

This is one of the most common members of the finch family in Ecuador, especially in agricultural areas of the highlands, mostly at 1,000–3,500m. The female lacks the male's black hood, but she does have the same bright yellow band in the wing as he does. Confusingly, several other species are very similar to this one, notably the Olivaceous Siskin, *C. olivacea,* of the foothills of the eastern Andean slope, where it is usually found in forest at about 900–1,700m elevation. The Saffron Siskin, *C. siemiradzkii,* occurs in the lowlands of the south-west, but that species has a brighter, plain golden-olive mantle.

137

GLOSSARY

Axillaries The feathers at the base of the underwing.

Bird wave A flock of birds travelling and feeding together.

Brood parasites Certain birds that lay their eggs in the nests of other birds and do not provide any parental care for their offspring.

Cap Well-defined patch of colour or bare skin on top of the head.

Cere An area of skin surrounding the nostrils, at the base of the upper mandible and beak.

Crepuscular Most active at dawn and dusk.

Diurnal Active during the day (in reference to typically nocturnal birds).

Endemic Restricted or confined to a specific country or region.

Eye-ring Area immediately surrounding the eye.

Eye-stripe A concolourous line running through the eye.

Flight feathers The primary, secondary and tail feathers.

Genus A group of species more closely related than a family.

Invertebrates Animals without backbones including insects, molluscs and spiders. Marine invertebrates include such animals as crabs, shrimps and shellfish.

Lore In birds, the surface on each side of the head between the eye and the upper base of the beak.

Mandible The upper and lower mandibles comprise the bill or beak of a bird.

Mollusc A soft-bodied invertebrate that usually has a hard, protective shell, such as a snail, limpet or mussel.

Mantle The upper back feathers.

Moult The shedding of old feathers and growth of new ones.

Montane Of or inhabiting mountainous country.

Moustachial stripe A streak extending backwards and downwards from the base of the bill.

Páramo Neotropical ecosystem located in the high elevations of the northern Andes between the upper forest line (*c.* 3,100m) and permanent snow line (*c.* 5,000m).

Primary feathers Flight feathers of the outer wing joint.

Riverine Of, relating to or situated on a river or riverbank.

Sallies/sallying Sudden flight from perch to catch prey or take fruit.

Saltado Mineral salt lick used by many forest birds, such as parrots, which rely largely on fruit in their diet. The salt helps balance the acidity in the fruit.

Secondary feathers Flight feathers of the inner portion of the wing.

Species A group of individuals with the same characteristics, which reproduce with each other.

Supercilium The eyebrow, or region of the eyebrow in birds.

Territorial Defending a particular area in order to protect a resource such as food, nest or display area.

Várzea Seasonally flooded forest lying next to rivers in the Amazon forest.

Wing coverts Small feathers that cover the bases of the primary and secondary feathers.

FURTHER READING

Books

Fjeldsa, Jon and Niels Krabbe, *Birds of the High Andes*, Zoological Museum, University of Copenhagen and Apollo Books, Svendborg, Denmark, 1990.

Hilty, Steven L. and William L. Brown, *A Guide to the Birds of Colombia*, Princeton University Press, 1986.

Restall, Robin, *et al.*, *Birds of Northern South America, An Identification Guide*, 2 Volumes, Christopher Helm, 2006.

Ridgely, Robert and Guy Tudor, *The Birds of South America: Oscine Passerines*, Texas University Press, 1989.

Ridgely, Robert and Guy Tudor, *The Birds of South America: the Sub-Oscine Passerines*, Oxford University Press, 1994.

Ridgely, Robert S. and Paul J. Greenfield, *The Birds of Ecuador*, 2 Volumes, Christopher Helm, 2001.

Williams, Robert J., *et al.*, *A Guide to Bird-watching in Ecuador and the Galapagos Islands*, Biosphere Publications, 2006.

Periodicals

Neotropical Bird Club, *Cotinga* (twice-yearly journal).

Neotropical Bird Club, *Neotropical Birding* (annual magazine).

ACKNOWLEDGEMENTS

I wish to thank the photographers who contributed a large number of fine photographs of great birds and put many of my own to shame. Phil Palmer at www.birdholidays.co.uk, and Vaughan Ashby at www.birdfinders.co.uk deserve my particular gratitude for the number of images they supplied. I also thank Jim Walford, Ron Hoff and Colin Bushell for their lovely pictures that grace the pages of this book. A big nod in the direction of Steven Hilty, whose wonderful, ground-breaking book *Birds of Colombia* was the only useful book when I first visited Ecuador many years ago. Hats off also to Robert Ridgely and Guy Tudor for producing the two fabulous volumes of *The Birds of South America*, and likewise to Robert Ridgely and Paul Greenfield for producing *The Birds of Ecuador*, both of which were mammoth tasks.

Special respect to the late Paul Coopmans for his friendship, ears and mind, and for simply being the legend that was Paul Coopmans. This book is dedicated to his memory.

Thanks to Xavier Munoz at Neblina Forest for his kind offers and all the good work he does. Also to Jim Hackett and his wife Maria, who employed me to entertain them and to show Jim lots of birds on various South American 'adventures'; to William Perez, who is also now at Neblina, and who was such a great help to me when I visited Kapawi with Jim. Thanks go to Eustace Barnes for his expert advice. My gratitude to Caento (Sam Padilla) for being such irritating but quite amusing company while driving Zodiacs on the Amazon – but especially for forcing the authorities to hand over the land rights to his Waorani people, thus enabling them to protect their forest home and empowering them to take control of their rightful inheritance. Thanks also to the people I have forgotten to thank – and sorry about that!

Last but not least, thanks to Krystyna Mayer and Simon Papps at New Holland for their incredible patience.

INDEX

140

141

143